Tax Guide 401

RENTAL REAL ESTATE

by

Holmes F. Crouch
Tax Specialist

Published by

Allyear Tax Guides

**20484 Glen Brae Drive
Saratoga, CA 95070**

ISBN 0-944817-53-X

LCCN 98-70248

Printed in U.S.A.

Series 400
Owners & Sellers

Tax Guide 401

RENTAL REAL ESTATE

For other titles in print, see page 224.

The author: **Holmes F. Crouch**
For more about the author, see page 221.

PREFACE

If you are a knowledge-seeking **taxpayer** looking for information, this book can be helpful to you. It is designed to be read — from cover to cover — in less than eight hours. Or, it can be "skim-read" in about 30 minutes.

Either way, you are treated to **tax knowledge** . . . *beyond the ordinary*. The "beyond" is that which cannot be found in IRS publications, FedWorld on-line services, tax software programs, Internet chatrooms, or E-mail bulletins.

Taxpayers have different levels of interest in a selected subject. For this reason, this book starts with introductory fundamentals and progresses onward. You can verify the progression by chapter and section in the table of contents. In the text, "applicable law" is quoted in pertinent part. Key phrases and key tax forms are emphasized. Real-life examples are given . . . in down-to-earth style.

This book has 12 chapters. This number provides depth without cross-subject rambling. Each chapter starts with a head summary of meaningful information.

To aid in your skim-reading, informative diagrams and tables are placed strategically throughout the text. By leafing through page by page, reading the summaries and section headings, and glancing at the diagrams and tables, you can get a good handle on the matters covered.

Effort has been made to update and incorporate all of the latest tax law changes that are *significant* to the title subject. However, "beyond the ordinary" does not encompass every conceivable variant of fact and law that might give rise to protracted dispute and litigation. Consequently, if a particular statement or paragraph is crucial to your own specific case, you are urged to seek professional counseling. Otherwise, the information presented is general and is designed for a broad range of reader interests.

The Author

INTRODUCTION

If you own or co-own, or expect to own or co-own, rental real estate, there are special tax benefits — and tax limitations — that await you. By "rental real estate" we mean property which is acquired primarily for its income-producing potential throughout its period of holding. The type of rental use — residential, commercial, or farming — is irrelevant with respect to the long-term investment advantages of such property.

For income-producing real estate, there are various "tax blessings" embedded in the Internal Revenue Code. Among these are—

1. Partial recovery of acquisition cost while the property is being held (via depreciation allowance).
2. Allowable expense deductions from income before tax netting (exclusive of improvements).
3. Long-term capital gain potential.
4. Opportunity for tax deferred exchanges.
5. Installment sales with ongoing interest income.

To be classed as income-producing realty, at least 85% of the tenant-usable space must be offered and available for rent . . . at all reasonable times. Furthermore, the property must be offered for rent to the general public on a continuing and ongoing basis, from date of acquisition to date of disposition. Otherwise, special rules trip in to limit the offsetting of losses against other sources of income. We have a lot to tell about these special rules.

The income from all rental real estate is reported on **Schedule E (Form 1040)**. On this schedule, there are approximately 15 expense-allowable offsets. Depending on which expenses are applicable in your case, the gross rental income may be reduced to a net loss. It is for this reason that the official title of Schedule E is: **Supplemental Income and Loss.**

While much can be said favorable to rental real estate, there is one dark side to it. Commencing in 1987, all rental realty is now automatically tax-classed as a **passive activity**. This means that stringent loss limitation rules apply, namely: **Section 469** of the

Internal Revenue Code. We devote an entire chapter to this 5,000-word tax code section. In other chapters, when pertinent, we keep reminding you of the loss limitations.

The essence of Section 469 is that all passive activity losses are summarily disallowed. Of course, there are some exceptions. The foremost exception — a new one commencing in 1994 — applies to *real estate professionals*. These are persons who devote the greater of 750 hours or 50% of their personal service time to real estate trades or businesses. There is also a "small taxpayer" exception which permits up to $25,000 to be used against other sources of income. Otherwise, any unallowable and unused passive losses can be carried forward until some parcel of property is sold in a fully taxable transaction.

There is still another dark side you should know about. When rental property is sold or otherwise disposed of, there is what is called: *depreciation recapture*. Often this is a big surprise to inexperienced owners. While the property was being used, cost-recovery depreciation helped to shelter some of the rental income from tax. When the property is transferred to a new owner, all previously allowed depreciation is recaptured as "ordinary gain."

With some ingenuity, the tax can be deferred on recapture gain. This requires a like-kind exchange in which other similar-in-use property is acquired. Such a transaction is called a "Section 1031 exchange." We have a whole chapter on this one subject alone. Although Section 1031 exchanges can go on indefinitely, there comes a time when you want to phase out of your rental activities, so as to enjoy the fruits thereof. On this, we have some interesting nuggets for you.

All along the way, though, there are many applicable tax forms and computer-matching details which — if unheeded — can spoil your investment successes. You are particularly vulnerable if you are involved in vacation home rentals, shared equity rentals, farmland rentals, out-of-state rentals, and co-ownership rentals.

In summary, we have tried to cover in this book the whole gamut of rental real estate activities (and their tax consequences) which you may not realize exist.

CONTENTS

Chapter	Page

11. INSTALLMENT SALES 11-1

12. OTHER DISPOSITIONS................. 12-1

1

IMPORTANT BASICS

Rental Real Estate Is Tax Distinguished From Other Forms Of Realty In Several Important Respects. Foremost: There Is No Social Security Tax (No "Second Tax") On Rental Income, As In The Case Of Trade Or Business Income. Because Of No Second Tax, Rental Realty Is Classed As "Passive Activity." As Such, Section 469 Applies: DISALLOWANCE OF PASSIVE LOSSES. However, There Are Three Exceptions. Exception 1 [Sec. 469(c)(7)] Applies To "Real Estate Professionals." Exception 2 [Sec. 469(i)] Applies To "Small Taxpayers." Exception 3 [Sec. 469(g)] Applies To Dispositions In A "Fully Taxable Transaction."

Everybody knows what "real estate" is. It is **land** . . . and improvements thereto. Land has been around for thousands of years, and in all likelihood will be around for thousands of years more. Therefore, it is *real*; it is something you can see, feel, shape, and build on.

Land is also an *estate*. This is because some person or entity has to own the land in order to use, enjoy, and be responsible for it. An estate evolves because the ownership of land can be passed on to assignees, heirs, and legatees . . . in perpetuity.

Improvements to land consist of buildings, structures, roadways, utilities, landscaping, recreational areas, storage facilities, and other "attachments" thereto. These improvements can be rented to others who are not the owners thereof. In the renting process, *income* accrues to the realty owner(s). Thus, rental real estate is property which is held primarily for the production of income on an ongoing basis.

In this chapter we want to lay the foundation for what constitutes "rental realty" and how it is tax-distinguished from other kinds of real estate. The distinctions exclude property used by owners for personal and family living, for conducting an active trade or business, or held primarily for sale to customers. Rental real estate is that which is actually being rented — or intended to be rented — to others for whatever use is authorized under state and local law.

Ownership & Title

The usable land mass of the 50 United States consists of nearly 2 billion acres (1,938,000,000 acres to be more precise). Of this acreage, approximately 25% is owned by various Federal, state, and local government agencies. This leaves approximately 1,450,000,000 acres (1.45 billion) which are "privatized." Private ownership is that which is titled in the names of persons or entities. Persons are human beings; entities are legal beings.

Ownership of land (and its improvements) consists of a "bundle of rights." Among these rights are its use, access, exclusion of nonowners, exploitation, and severalty. Different rights to the same realty can be owned by different owners. For example, the improvements can be owned by one owner; the surface can be owned by another owner; and the subsurface can be owned by still another owner. Diversity of realty ownership is called fragmentation of rights. The degree of fragmentation depends on the diversity of rights recognized by the legal system where the land is located.

All privatized land in the U.S. is segmented into unequal-sized parcels. A "parcel" may be as small as 1/10th of an acre (or less) to as large as 10,000 acres (or more). Each parcel is identified by a legal description of its boundaries, location, rights, and indexing to the "maps" of the political jurisdiction of its situs. In some jurisdictions, indexing is by the assignment of an APN: Assessor's Parcel Number. The Assessor, of course, is the property-taxing agency for the county of situs.

Title to each parcel of land is evidenced by an instrument called a *deed.* Functionally, a deed is a written instrument for the transfer of ownership from a prior owner (grantor) to a new owner (grantee). In principle, all ownerships can be traced back to a discoverer, conqueror, sovereign, or some other "first owner." This is the role of title searching by land title companies which assures the accuracy and legality of ownership by each new owner. The ownership of all land within a given political jurisdiction is recorded in Official Records of the county where the property itself is located.

Recordation of Ownership

Why is the introductory narrative above important to the subject of this book?

It is important because the IRS (Internal Revenue Service) looks to the owner of rental realty for all federal tax accounting and tax liability. State and local agencies also look to the owner for tax and legal-service purposes. The "owner" is that name, names, or entity listed as the *grantee* on whatever title evidence is recorded in public records. Therefore, recordation of ownership becomes an essential "first step" in understanding the tax treatment of rental property.

Proper recordation of ownership is evidenced by the following sequence of events:

One. The title instrument (deed) is acknowledged and notarized by a public witness who attests to the actual signature(s) of the grantor(s).

Two. The title instrument is submitted to the Recorder's Office at the administrative center having jurisdiction over all land within its political borders.

Three. Recordation is signified by the assignment of an Instrument Number and by designation of the Book and Page of the official records where the instrument is recorded. The recordation occurs on the date and time stamped in the upper right-hand corner of the title instrument.

Four. Upon recordation, the title instrument becomes a public record where it is subject to inspection and review by anyone having an interest in or curiosity concerning it.

Most pertinent to our discussion is any curiosity of the IRS with respect to ownership matters and responsibilities. Neither all rental owners nor all IRS agents know the essential elements that constitute a valid recorded title. It is for this reason that we present Figure 1.1. We depict only the key elements that one should look for when appraising the ownership aspects of realty being rented, or being sold or exchanged after being rented.

Recording Requested By —————————— When Recorded Mail To: —————————— ——————————	Recorder's Data ● Instrument No. —————— ● Date & time —————— ● Where recorded —————— ● Book & Page —————— ● Recorder's name ——————

GRANT DEED

For valuable consideration, etc. ....
GRANTOR(S) ———— *Full legal name(s) and*
——————————— *prior ownership form*

hereby GRANT to
GRANTEE(S) ————— *Full legal name(s) and*
——————————— *current ownership form*

General Description ———— *Location, nature of*
——————————— *improvements, address, etc.*

County of Situs ———— *City, County, State*

Parcel No. ———— *Assessor's index*
Legal Description ———— *Lot No., Tract No., Map No.,*
——————————— *Volume No., Surveyor's*
——————————— *directions & dimensions*

Exepting Therefrom ———— *Restrictions and*
——————————— *reserved rights*

IN WITNESS WHEREOF ———— *Date of execution*
——————————— *& signature of GRANTOR(S)*

Subscribed and Sworn
to Before ———— *Place of execution*
——————————— *Name, official seal, and expiration*
——————————— *of commission of Notary Public*

Fig. 1.1 - Elements of Recorded Title to Property

In Figure 1.1, the grantor is the prior legal owner of the subject realty; the grantee is the current legal owner. The IRS is interested in both the grantor and grantee. The grantor has made a capital transaction for which a gross proceeds reporting to the IRS is required. The grantee has acquired a capital asset for which its rental income must be reported to the IRS each year that it is being so held. Consequently, care must be taken to assure that the grantor and grantee names are complete and accurate in all respects. This includes an alias ("aka": also known as), if any. The full legal names of the grantor and grantee are just as important as the full legal description of the property involved.

Specificity Among Co-Owners

In the same manner that ownership rights can be fragmented, so, too, can ownership interests. An "interest" is the fraction of 100% of ownership rights where there is more than one individual owner. Rental realty can be owned by one, two, three, five, or more co-owners. When there is more than one owner, the fractional ownership of each co-owner must be indicated with specificity.

One individual grantee may be the 100% owner of rental property. If so, the title instrument (using purely fictitious names) designates such person as—

> John J. Jones OR (Mary M. Milder)
> *a single man* (*a single woman*)
> OR, *an unmarried man* (OR, *an unmarried woman*)

The term "single" implies that the owner has never been married. The term "unmarried" implies that the owner was married at one time, but is currently divorced or widowed.

When identifying individual persons on a title instrument, the marital status, if any, needs to be made clear. State and local family law and inheritance matters require this clarity.

This is not to say that a married person cannot own rental property 100% in his or her own right. If a married person does indeed own 100% of the property separately from his/her spouse, the grantee description may read as—

> John J. Jones
> *a married man as his sole and separate property*,
> OR

Mary M. Milder,
a married woman as her sole and separate property.

Otherwise, for IRS purposes, a married couple is treated as each owning 50% of the subject property. If they file a "married joint" return (Form 1040), the 50/50 presumption is irrelevant. But if they file "married separate" returns, absent a retitling of the property, each is regarded as 50% co-owner. This IRS presumption prevails whether the realty is titled as community property, tenants by the entirety (in non-community states), or joint tenancy. For tax purposes, husband and wife are generally treated as one taxpayer/owner.

Rental property, of course, can be co-owned by other than husband and wife. It can be co-owned by father and son(s), mother and daughter(s), brother(s) and sister(s), family and friends, investors and associates, each of whom may be married or not. Other than for practical reasons, there is no limit to the number of co-owners that may be involved. As a general rule, though, when there are more than five co-owners, it is preferable that the grantee be in the name of some entity, such as partnership, corporation, or trust. The entity agreement will then specify the exact fractional ownership of each participating co-owner. Entity ownership introduces other tax ramifications, which we prefer to sidestep entirely.

For five or less co-owners, the preferable grantee title form is *tenants-in-common*. As tenants-in-common, each co-owner's fractional interest can be specified precisely. For example, Owner A may have a 29.64% interest, Owner B a 25.15% interest, Owner C a 20.80%, Owner D a 14.56%, and Owner E a 9.85% interest. (Total = 100%.) As tenants-in-common, each co-owner (and his spouse or heir) has a valid legal claim to the indicated percentage of the property. Otherwise, if the percentages are not indicated, it is tax presumed that they are co-equal owners.

Typical Rental Uses

The most common form of rental property is that which is used for *residential* purposes. There can be single-family rentals, duplex rentals, triplex rentals, 4-plex rentals, and on up to 100 or more multi-unit rental complexes. In all cases, a rental "unit" is a separate living arrangement for eating, sleeping, entertaining, raising children, and sanitation. The lifestyles involved will depend on the economics of each zoning district and on the social and occupational ambitions of the inhabitants thereof. Yet, the tax treatment of each dwelling unit is much the same.

There are also extensive rental units for *nonresidential* purposes. These are workplace units rather than dwelling units. The gamut includes professional offices, commercial buildings, retail shops, repair shops, industrial plants, warehousing facilities, public storage lockers, and so on. Depending on the occupational scale involved, the bulk of nonresidential facilities is owned by entities rather than by five or less individuals.

Farms and farmland also can be rented. A "farm" typically consists of a dwelling unit (or several dwellings) plus multiple structures for housing crops and equipment. The owner of a farm may rent it out in its entirety, or he may sharecrop it with those living and working on the farm.

Bare land is also a source of rental income. The land can be rented for grazing purposes, for hunting and recreation, for parking vehicles, and for camping and mobile home sites.

Shallow-water "land" is rentable when docks and moorings are built and rented to boat owners and other sportsmen.

In all rental cases, the improvements to land are subject to "wear and tear" by the tenants thereon. For this wear and tear, a *depreciation deduction* against the rental income is allowed. This deduction is a major tax attribute of rental real estate. We'll go into considerable detail on depreciation matters in Chapter 2. In the meantime, there are other tax attributes you should know about.

The "Second Tax" Distinction

Rental real estate is distinguished from other forms of real estate in that there is no social security/medicare tax on the income therefrom. There is regular income tax, of course. But there is no "second tax" on the same income. The tax for social security and medicare is *in addition to* one's regular tax on income. It is a combined flat rate of approximately 15% on the first dollar of income . . . and upwards.

Income from rental property is generated primarily by the property itself. It is the use of the property that produces the income: not the personal services or intellect of the owner(s) thereof. The social security/medicare tax applies to all personal service income. It would be inappropriate, therefore, to apply this tax to the impersonality of buildings, structures, and land.

The personal attention and services of the owner(s) of rental realty are required only occasionally and intermittently. Yes, there are rent checks and security deposits to collect once a month or so; there are rental and lease agreements to sign once a year or so; and there are some repairs and refurbishments to be made from time to time. But, by and large, the paying tenants take care of themselves. They clean and maintain their own spaces; they pay for most of their own utilities; and they provide their own furnishings. Except for complaints, the owner is mostly out of sight.

Contrast this degree of activity with that of hotel or motel owner. The owner of a hotel/motel has to manage and be present on his property on a *daily basis*. Paying guests arrive and depart daily. There is food, maid, and luggage service to be provided. There are phone calls to answer and make; there are billing statements to be prepared; and there are special requests and functions that require ongoing attention. Because of the daily and ongoing personal attention and services required, the owners of hotel/motel property pay social security tax — the second tax — on their net incomes. They are in an active trade or business of providing hotel/motel services. Active trade or business income is social security taxed.

Another trade or business twist is that of a real estate broker. He acquires "listings" and "inventories" of realty which he offers for sale to the general public. Although, in a sense, he is holding property for the production of income, it is not rental income property. There is no income (to the broker) while the property is being held. The income is generated when the listed property is sold. The result is that the broker pays both types of taxes — regular and social security — on his income.

As another real property variant, suppose a rental property owner has a 20-unit apartment building. He decides to convert the dwelling units into condominiums and sell them one at a time. Is he in the trade or business of developing, converting, and selling condominiums? Or, is such effort just an extension of his rental business?

Answer: He is in the business of converting rental units into condominiums. He pays the second tax (social security) on the income therefrom. Particularly so, if he terminated all rental agreements at approximately the same time, and took on an active role in the conversion development and sales.

So important is this distinction of no second tax, that we present a depiction of it in Figure 1.2. IRS Regulation 1.469-1T(e)(3) points out that rental realty is characterized by the "average period"

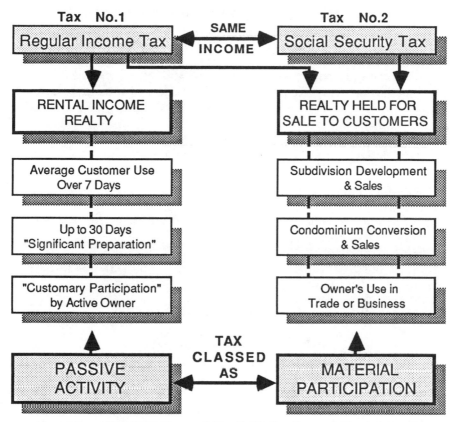

Fig. 1.2 - The "No Second Tax" Distinction of Rental Realty

of customer use being more than seven days. The regulation also permits significant personal services by the owner(s) if performed over a period of 30 days or less, for the express purpose of making the property available for use by customers. Awareness of Regulation 1.469-1T(e)(3) is important for avoiding tripping into application of the second tax.

Classed as "Passive Activity"

Rental real estate is that which is held primarily for the production of income . . . on an annual basis. This is not to say that the property cannot eventually be sold to earn further income. It's just that its primary purpose is to produce rental income for the owner, without the owner taking an active daily role in generating that income. This absence of material participation causes such property to be IRS-classed as *passive activity* property. This is so indicated in Figure 1.2.

The tax law on point is Section 469(c): **Passive Activity Defined**. Pertinent excerpts from this section of the Revenue Code are—

> *The term "passive activity" includes any rental activity . . . in which the taxpayer does not materially participate.*

The term "rental activity" means—

> *any activity where payments are principally for the use of tangible property.* [Sec. 469(j)(8).]

And, as per Section 469(h)(1), the term "material participation" means an activity in which the taxpayer participates—

> *on a regular, continuous, and substantial basis.*

Why are we telling you about Section 469?

Because, since there is no social security tax to pay, there is a limit to the amount of expenses you can use for offsetting your rental income. For passive activities, your expense offsets are limited to the amount of income generated from each activity. In other words, for regular income tax purposes, you cannot produce a net (aggregate) rental loss for the year. (There are three exceptions which we'll explain below.)

The general rule on point is Section 469(a): **Passive Activity Losses Limited**. This rule reads in part as—

> *(a)*   *Disallowance*
> *(1)* ***In general***. *If for any taxable year, the taxpayer is* [an individual], *neither—*
> *(A) the passive activity loss, nor*
> *(B) the passive activity credit,*
> *for the taxable year shall be allowed.*

Section 469(a) — the "general disallowance" rule — pretty well dampens incentive for using rental real estate for tax sheltering purposes. Ordinarily, a tax shelter produces a net loss which can be used to offset other positive sources of income (many of which are subject to the second tax). If bona fide, the disallowed losses are not totally lost; they are "suspended."

Real Estate Professionals

The foremost exception to the general disallowance rule of Section 469(a) pertains to real estate professionals. These are property owners who "materially participate" in their rental real estate activities as well as in other activities associated with real estate.

To qualify as a real estate professional, a person must devote—

1. more than 50% of his personal service time during the year to real property trades or businesses, which constitutes
2. more than 750 hours . . . at least.

A "real property trade or business" is defined by subsection 469(c)(7)(C) as—

any real property development, redevelopment, construction, reconstruction, acquisition, conversion, rental, operation, management, leasing, or brokerage [thereof].

This exception is designated in the tax code as Section 469(c)(7): *Special rules for taxpayers in real property business.* Here, the term "taxpayer" applies to an individual, to a closely held corporation or to a 5% employee-owner of a business entity whether incorporated or not. In the case of a corporation, more than 50% of its gross receeipts must derive from real property trades or businesses. In the case of a married couple filing a joint return, one spouse or the other must meet the more-than-50% **and** more-than-750-hour personal service requirements.

Upon meeting these requirements, the qualifying person or entity is treated as being actively engaged in the real estate business. As such, the passive loss disallowance rule — Section 469(a) — does not apply. This means that, provided there is also active participation in *rental* real estate activities, the net losses from the rental activities can be used to offset other sources of income . . . without limit. This special exception applies to tax years beginning 1994 and thereafter [IRC Sec. 469(c)(7).]

The $25,000 Offset Exception

The second exception to the general disallowance rule is the "small taxpayer" exception. This is also known as the $25,000 offset. This is the amount of passive losses that can be used to offset other sources of nonrealty income, provided such income is within certain limits.

For purposes of Section 469(a), a small taxpayer is one (together with spouse) whose adjusted gross income for a given taxable year (without the rental loss exception) is less than $150,000. The full exception is allowed for gross incomes of $100,000 or less. Between $100,000 and $150,000 a "phase-out" portion is allowed. That is, the phase-out is a reduction of the exception by 50 percent of the amount in excess of $100,000.

The small taxpayer exception amount is $25,000 of net rental loss each year. In Section 469(i), this is designated as the ***$25,000 Offset for Rental Real Estate Activities***. In pertinent part, this tax code section reads as follows:

> *In the case of any natural person, subsection (a) shall not apply to that portion of the passive activity loss . . . for any taxable year which is attributable to all rental real estate activities with respect to which such individual actively participated in such taxable year. . . . The aggregate amount to which* [this exception] *applies for any taxable year shall not exceed $25,000.*

In the official wording above, there are three conditions for allowability of the $25,000 loss exception. One, only *natural persons* are eligible. Entities such as partnerships, corporations, or trusts are not eligible. This is why we have purposely limited our focus in this book to five individual co-owners or less. The $25,000 passive loss exception is a powerful tax attribute.

The second condition for eligibility is that the natural persons **actively participate** in the rental activities. For this purpose, "active participation" is far short of material participation which defines applicability of the second tax (social security) on trade or business income. Active participation is simply that which an individual owner of rental property would customarily do in overseeing the collection of rental income and general maintenance of his property. Absentee owners who never visit their property, or who never see the rent checks as they come in, are intentionally excluded from the $25,000 loss exception.

The third condition for the $25,000 offset is that it is the *aggregate loss* for all rental properties of the owner(s). If there were five separate properties, for example, the $25,000 offset would have to be shared proportionately among all loss properties. For this sharing, a "property" is a separate parcel of land and improvements which has been officially titled and recorded. A property may consist of any number of dwelling units so long as they are contained on one parcel, separately recorded.

In Figure 1.3, we depict the $25,000 loss offset as it applies to the aggregate of all properties owned (and co-owned) by a given taxpayer. The relative roles of full exclusion and phase-out exclusion are also shown. Any aggregate losses in excess of $25,000 are suspended until each allocable property is disposed of, by sale or otherwise.

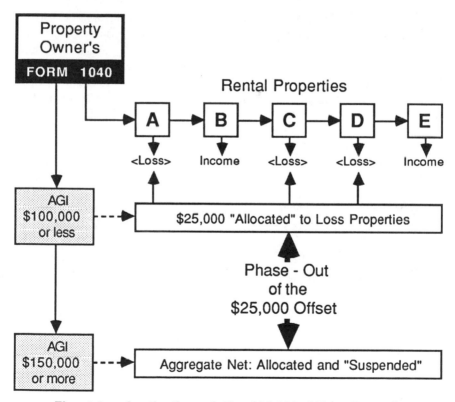

Fig. 1.3 - Application of the $25,000 Offset Exception

Suspended Losses

The phrase "suspended losses" refers to the disallowed (passive activity) losses in a given year which are allowed to be carried over to the following taxable year (or years). It is in this sense that the unallowed losses are suspended. The tax law on point is Section 469(b).

Section 469(b) is titled: *Disallowed Loss Carried to Next Year.* This subsection reads in full as—

Except as otherwise provided in this section, any loss or credit from an activity which is disallowed under subsection (a) shall be treated as a deduction or credit allocable to such activity in the next taxable year. [Emphasis added.]

In the wording above, particularly note the emphasized phrase: "allocable to such activity . . ." in the next taxable year. This means that each rental property which has a disallowed loss has to keep track of its own "allocable" suspended losses. The disallowed losses cannot be aggregated and assigned to whichever carryover year property gives the best tax offset. Suspended loss accounting is a *property by property* affair.

For example, you have three rental properties: A, B, and C. Property A produces a net loss of <$18,500>; Property B produces a net income of $3,500; and Property C produces a net loss of <$15,000>. How much are your suspended losses, and how are they allocated to each property?

The aggregate losses are <$18,500> plus <$15,000>, or <$33,500>. The aggregate positive income is $3,500. Thus, the disallowed loss is <$30,000> [<$33,500> + 3,500]. Assume that $25,000 of this loss qualifies for the exception.

The $33,500 aggregate loss is allocated as follows:

Property	Actual Loss	Allocable Fraction	Allocable Loss	Sec. 469(i) Exception	Suspended Loss
A	18,500	0.5522	1,933	13,805	2,761
C	15,000	0.4478	1,567	11,195	2,239
Totals	33,500	1.0000	3,500	25,000	5,000

The carryover allocation applies to the loss properties only: not to the positive net income properties. The income properties simply reduce the aggregate amount of actual loss that is suspended and carried over.

The far right column above illustrates how the carryover losses are reduced by the $25,000 offset exception. This exception reduces the net loss carryover to $5,000. There is still one more exception. Recall that Section 469(b) starts out with the phrase: *Except as otherwise provided.*

Entire Interest Dispositions

The third exception to the passive loss disallowance rule occurs when an owner (or co-owner) disposes of his entire interest in the rental property. The disposition may be by any fully tax accountable transaction, such as: cash sale, installment sale, death, foreclosure, or other "final" disposition. When this happens, all gain or loss is tax recognized, including all cumulative suspended losses.

The tax law on point is Section 469(g): *Dispositions of Entire Interest in Passive Activity.* This section is worded ambiguously. By judicious excerpting, it reads as—

> *If during the taxable year a taxpayer disposes of his entire interest in any passive activity (or former passive activity), the following rule shall apply:*
> *(1) Fully taxable transaction. If all gain or loss realized on such disposition is recognized, the excess of the sum of any loss from such activity for such taxable year (determined after application of subsection (b) [above], plus any loss realized on such disposition, over the net income or gain for such taxable year from all passive activities . . . shall be treated as a loss which is not from a passive activity.* [Emphasis added.]

We warned you that the official wording is ambiguous. But if you reread the emphasized last clause, a key tax point comes through. All prior and current disallowed losses (for the property being disposed of) are recharacterized as *nonpassive* losses and allowed in full. The only precondition is that the allocable current-year loss be computed (in its relationship to all properties) before adding it to the cumulative prior-year carryovers, for computing the disposition gain or loss.

Using Carryovers Strategically

Subsection 469(b) — carryover of disallowed losses — and subsection 469(g) — disposition of entire interest — are particularly advantageous for the serious property owner with long-term profit motives. Such a person is one who has an ownership interest of *10% or more* in each rental property, and who reasonably participates in its overall management. For such individuals, the loss carryovers become a strategic tax planning opportunity.

The strategic use of loss carryovers, cumulatively year after year, requires that you own (or co-own) multiple rental properties. By "multiple," we mean between three and five properties (approximately). With this number of properties, the idea is to establish a rollover cycle. That is, every other year or so, one property is disposed of and another rental property is acquired. You pick that property which has the largest cumulative loss carryovers, and you dispose of it in a taxable transaction. After all, do you intend to hold on to all of your properties forever?

Tax planning-wise, you should hold the to-be-disposed-of property from three to five years. This is to allow sufficient market appreciation to accrue and to allow significant carryover losses to build up. This way, during every holding year, you can claim the maximum benefits to which you are entitled. You can do this without worrying about Section 469(a) disallowances. This, really, is what this book is all about.

When we get to Chapters 10, 11, and 12, we'll present alternative ways for tax beneficial rollovers. A point to keep in mind in this regard is the role of depreciation recapture in your disposition planning. As you'll see in the next and subsequent chapters, depreciation is a cost recovery allowance which, together with other expense deductions, can create a net rental loss. When the property is sold, depreciation recapture becomes a virtual guarantee for producing tax accountable gain.

2

DEPRECIATION ALLOWANCE

Depreciation Is An "Allowed/Allowable" Wear-And-Tear Deduction Against The Rental Income Of Realty, Other Than The Land Itself. It Is The RECOVERY Of Your Capital Investment Over Prescribed Periods Of Time. Section 168 Prescribes 9 Classes Of Property With Statutory Useful-Life "Spreads." 3-, 5-, 7-, And 10-Year Property May Use The 200% DB (Declining Balance) Method; 15- and 20-Year May Use 150% DB. Residential And Nonresidential Realty Must Use Straight Line Over 27.5 and 39 Years, Respectively. Each Property Owner Must Set Up And Maintain His Own Depreciation Schedules For Continuous "Tax Basis" Accounting.

The depreciation allowance for improvements to real estate is a tax subject that has been around for a long time. Owners and fractional owners of rental property are quite familiar with the deduction of depreciation against the income therefrom. As the Supreme Court stated in 1943 (*Detroit Edison Co. vs Commissioner IRS*; 319 US 98)—

A depreciable asset in its lifetime must pay for itself, before it can be said to pay anything to its owner.

The tax concept of depreciation bears no relationship to any decline in market value. It is *not* the opposite of "appreciation." It is an element of physical exhaustion and obsolescence due to use and the passage of time. Indeed, the value of a realty asset may increase with time (due to inflation, upscaling of the area, access location), yet the buildings and structures themselves may actually "wear out."

For tax purposes, depreciation is the process of spreading the cost or other basis of an asset over its useful life. This is the theory, at least. But, as you'll learn in this chapter, the tax rules for depreciation accounting are not as simple as theory suggests. For each parcel of property there has to be a separate depreciation schedule or a *set* of depreciation schedules. There may be a subschedule for the building, a subschedule for its improvements, and a subschedule for other property items on the land which are not directly attached to the building structure. Good depreciation schedule-keeping can work wonders for tax basis updating.

Historically Confrontational

For some inexplicable reason — possibly "power mania" — the IRS has fought the depreciation concept for years. There is a whole raft of court cases on the subject; some in which the IRS won, and some in which the IRS lost. Particularly on realty structures, the IRS has taken the view that buildings and structures attached to land have virtually infinite life. Their argument goes that since land itself does not depreciate, anything attached to it should last forever.

The very first income tax laws were published in 1913. Even then, a "reasonable allowance" for depreciation was prescribed. Unfortunately, the IRS's concept of reasonableness and that of most taxpayers were worlds apart. As a result, over the years Congress has enacted five different sets of depreciation rules, namely:

1. GDS: General Depreciation System [1913-1953]
2. CLS: Class Life System [1954-1970]
3. ADR: Asset Depreciation Range [1971-1980]
4. ACRS: Accelerated Cost Recovery System [1981-1986]
5. MACRS: Modified Accelerated Cost Recovery [1987-?]

The whole idea behind all of these rules is to define and classify all depreciable assets by industry usage, irrespective of the variant uses and locations by individual taxpayers. This means that a housing structure in Barrow, Alaska, for example, would — by dictate — have the same class life and depreciation range as a similar structure in Hialeah, Florida. In other words, functionally similar realty structures anywhere in the world should have the same depreciable life. It was in this vein that the IRS forced the depreciation of realty structures into a range of 40 to 60 years of useful life. After all, aren't there still some 100-year-old buildings around?

The year 1981 was a rare moment in the taxation history of the U.S. Congress finally got enough courage to stand up to the IRS. Its courage was boosted by the fact that the U.S. was in a severe economic slump, and Congress wanted to get businesses going again. To do so, it redefined depreciation as a *cost recovery* process. It became a statutory right that businesses and rental owners be entitled to recover their eligible costs as rapidly as reasonable, without IRS interference.

Whereas, previous to 1981, the IRS had prescribed some 20 or so class lifetimes, the ACRS rules reduced this number to five property classes. New rental property was allowed to be depreciated over 15 years rather than 40. This "accelerated" the cost recovery process which, indeed, helped to boost the national economy.

Unfortunately, the 1981 ACRS rules spawned abuses by tax shelter promoters of real estate investments. New residential and nonresidential buildings were constructed more for their tax benefits than for their economic benefits. Congress corrected this situation in 1986 by enacting the MACRS legislation.

As the depreciation rules now stand, there are two basic tax laws in effect: Section 167 and Section 168. We cover the highlights of each of these two sections below. Both are currently operable.

Section 167: Old Law

Rental realty placed in service before 1981, and still in service, comes under Section 167: *Depreciation*. This section comprises approximately 5,000 words. This section has been amended and updated to cover post-1980 realty acquisitions, if a property owner so elects. Although we treat it as "old law," it is not obsolete by any means. Its rules are just more general in order to preserve the wear-and-tear depreciation concept.

The two most important portions of Section 167 are its subsections (a) and (c). Its subsection (a): *General Rule*, reads in full as follows:

There shall be allowed as a depreciation deduction a reasonable allowance for the exhaustion, wear and tear (including a reasonable allowance for obsolescence)—
  (1)   of property used in a trade or business, or
  (2)   of property held for the production of income.

On its surface, subsection 167(a) is certainly straight-forward enough. Its paragraph (2) clearly includes rental real estate: "property held for the production of income." This paragraph encompasses all forms of rental realty, such as residential buildings, nonresidential buildings, agricultural structures, aquatic structures, roads and utilities, fencing and landscaping, appliances and furniture, and improvements thereto.

Subsection 167(c): ***Basis for Depreciation***, reads in part as follows:

The basis on which exhaustion, wear and tear, and obsolescence are to be allowed in respect of any property shall be the adjusted basis provided in section 1011 [relating to adjustments in section 1012 through 1016] *for the purpose of determining the gain on the sale or other disposition of such property.*

Subsection (c) tells us two things. One is the hindsight principle for determining what depreciation is to be allowed many years after the property is acquired and placed in service. The second telemessage is that the depreciation allowance must be adjusted for recapture when determining *gain*— not loss — at time of sale. In other words, whatever depreciation you may have claimed during the period of holding your property is really only tentative. It is not fixed in concrete until after the property is sold (or otherwise disposed of).

As late as 1990, there was a total of 18 subsections comprising Section 167. On November 5, 1990 (Public Law 101-508), 13 of these subsections were either repealed, rescinded, or stricken. This left five subsections revised and shortened. We've quoted two of these, namely: subsections (a) and (c). Subsections (d) and (e) are not pertinent to our discussion. They focus on life estates, remainderman interests, and beneficiaries of trusts. In 1993 (P.L. 103-66), a subsection (f)(1) was reinstated. It addresses computer software by allowing straight line depreciation over a useful life of 36 months. The existing subsection (b): ***Cross Reference***, seems out of order. Nevertheless, it reads in full as—

For determination of depreciation deduction in case of property to which section 168 applies, see section 168.

The reference to Section 168 is the "new law" on depreciation which was enacted by the Tax Reform Act of 1986. This Act replaced the old concept of depreciation as being wear and tear, with the concept of *cost recovery* depreciation. Cost recovery is a more realistic view where obsolescence plays a major role in the usefulness of an item.

Section 168: New Law

Section 168 is titled: *Accelerated Cost Recovery System.* Although this section consists of approximately 8,000 words, it attempts to uniformize the rules by designating nine property classes, each with statutory recovery periods. We present these nine property classes in Figure 2.1. Note particularly that rental real estate *buildings* comprise Classes 7 and 8. The lesser life classes apply to those property items frequently "associated" with land, its uses, and its improvements.

Sec. 168 (a) : Applicable Recovery Periods (Post-'86)			
	Property Class	Recovery Period	Useful Life
1	3-year property	3 years	4 or less years
2	5-year property	5 years	4 to 10 years
3	7-year property	7 years	10 to 16 years
4	10-year property	10 years	16 to 20 years
5	15-year property	15 years	20 to 25 years
6	20-year property	20 years	25 or more years
7	Residential realty	27.5 years	30 to 40 years
8	Nonresidential realty	31.5 years	40 to 60 years
9	Railroad tunnels	50 years	60 or more years

Fig. 2.1 - The 9 Property Classes of Section 168

Subsection 168(a): *General Rule*, reads in full as—

Except as otherwise provided in this section, the depreciation deduction provided by section 167(a) for any tangible property shall be determined by using—
- *(1)   the applicable depreciation method,*
- *(2)   the applicable recovery period, and*
- *(3)   the applicable convention.*

Reference to the "applicable convention" relates to the placement-in-service period when depreciation begins and when it ends. For habitable real property — residential dwellings or nonresidential workplaces — the applicable convention is the mid-month convention [Sec. 168(d)(2)]. The mid-month convention is defined as—

A convention which treats all property placed in service during any month (or disposed of during any month) as placed in service (or disposed of) on the mid-point of such month. [Sec. 168(d)(4)(B).]

For realty assets other than habitable buildings, the half-year convention is used. This means that items placed in service anywhere between January 1 and December 31 are treated as eligible for six months' depreciation. However, if 40% or more of the depreciable assets are placed in service during the last three months of the year, the *mid-quarter* convention applies. The mid-quarter convention is far less advantageous than the half-year convention.

As to methods of depreciation, subsection 168(b)(3) restricts residential and nonresidential buildings to the straight-line method only. For other (nonhabitable) realty assets, the 200% DB (Declining Balance) or 150% DB methods may be used, switching to straight-line when advantageously appropriate.

Section 168 is applicable to all rental realty acquired and placed in service after 1986. It also addresses numerous other depreciable assets which are trade or business oriented and beyond the scope of our discussions.

There are two particularly nice *elective* features of Section 168 which are applicable to rental realty. One is subsection 168(b)(3)(D) which allows a property owner to switch to straight-line depreciation (for nonhabitable assets) any time he wants to do so. The other is subsection 168(g)(7)(A) which allows a property owner to stretch out his depreciation schedules to 40 years for habitable assets.

These two elections are important — and highly desirable — when you are up against the loss limitation rules and carryover suspensions required by Section 469.

Land: Nondepreciable, But—

Please glance back at Figure 2.1 for a moment. Do you see any depreciable class designation for land?

No; you do not. The nearest is a railroad grading or tunnel bore. Its recovery period is 50 years. Although such an item has no direct application to rental real estate, it does introduce an important distinction between land and its nonhabitable improvements.

Fundamentally, the concept of nondepreciability of land derives from its natural and pristine state. If left unattended and unused, it would stay in its natural state indefinitely. Yes, there could be erosion due to storms, floods, snowpacks, mudslides, earthquakes, and the like. But these are natural causes which are distinct from exhaustion and wear and tear due to income use. When the natural causes dissipate, the land reverts to some natural state in keeping with its inherent geography and topography.

The same reversion principle applies to nonhabitable improvements to land. Clearing, grading, and trenching land in order to construct improvements on it are part of the cost of the land: nondepreciable. So, too, would be landfill. If the improvements were abandoned or removed, the land itself would revert to some natural state.

Now, suppose you had previously acquired an 8-unit apartment building and decide to install an in-the-ground swimming pool. Would not the swimming pool, with its surrounding patio, its water-filling and purifying equipment, and its structural casings, be a depreciable asset?

Yes, certainly.

Ask yourself: If you abandoned the pool and its accessories, would the land revert to its natural state? No, it would remain disfigured. Much labor and effort would be required to remove the pool items and add landfill to restore it to its prepool natural state.

What would be the depreciable life of the pool?

It could be 15 or 20 years, depending on its design and climatic environment. The nearest tax rules on point are subsections 168(e)(3)(E) and (F). Paragraph (E) is 15-year property which includes . . . *any municipal wastewater treatment plant.* Paragraph (F) is 20-year property which includes . . . *any municipal sewers.*

While these items are not specifically identical to a private pool in an apartment complex, they are sufficiently analogous for authoritative reliance on the depreciable class lives prescribed.

What about landscaping, driveways, sidewalks, fencing, retaining walls, water wells, sprinkler systems, tennis courts, barbecue facilities, and so on? Are they part of the land? Or, are they improvements to land which would leave it disfigured, thereby preventing it from reverting to its natural state, were they to be abandoned?

They are improvements, of course. And they are depreciable.

Other than specific Tax Court cases on contested issues, the most analogous depreciable life classes are 7 years and 10 years: Subsections 168(e)(3)(C) and (D). Paragraph (C) defines 7-year property as—

(i)   *any railroad track,*
(ii)   *any property which does not have a class life, and is not otherwise classified.*

Paragraph (D) defines 10-year property as—

(i)   *any single purpose agricultural or horticultural structure,*
(ii)   *any tree or vine bearing fruit or nuts.*

Establishing "Land Fraction"

It is a long-established income tax principle that land in its natural state, or subject to reversion to such state, is not depreciable. We have no quarrel with this.

The question arises, though, when you acquire a parcel of land with improvements thereon, how do you establish what part is land and what part is improvements? In other words, what is the *land fraction* of an improved parcel?

In Chapter 1, we told you that all parcels of realty are recorded in the official records of the county of situs of the property. We also told you that each parcel of land is indexed to the official maps of the county, for property tax assessment purposes. All local jurisdictions are interested in your property for revenue purposes.

The revenue interest of local jurisdictions is exercised by assigning an "assessed value" to your land AND to your improvements. These two assessed values are separately stated in a document sent to you. This document, of course, is your Property

Tax Bill for the current fiscal year. Different values for land and improvements are used because different property tax rates apply to each. The more the improvements on a given parcel size, the more the local revenue generated.

Bear in mind that locally assessed values for property tax purposes are not necessarily true market-value appraisals. In fact, assessed values and market values may have no direct relationship to each other. Nevertheless, it is the *relative* assessed values of land and improvements that the IRS will accept as a means of establishing your land fraction.

For illustrative purposes, we present in Figure 2.2 the kind of assessment information that goes on a representative property tax bill. Note that we show example values as—

Land	$ 64,500
Improvements	150,000
Total Assessment	$215,000

PROPERTY TAX BILL	YEAR	COUNTY _____ STATE ____

Property Owner(s) _____

Parcel No. _____

Tax Rate Area _____

Property Address _____

Title Instrument No. _____

Taxing Agencies	Amount
●	$
●	
●	
●	
●	

ASSESSED VALUES $

■ Land.................. 64,500
■ Improvements......150,000
Total Value
Assessed 215,000

| Total Tax Due ▶ | $ |

| DUE DATES | 1st | $ |
| | 2nd | $ |

Assessment No. _____

Fig. 2.2 - Example Entries on Property Tax Statement

Using these example figures, the land fraction becomes—

$$\frac{\text{Land Assessment}}{\text{Total Assessment}} = \frac{64,500}{215,000} = 0.30 \text{ or } 30\%$$

You then apply this fraction to the *actual* acquisition cost or other basis of your property: land plus improvements. Suppose you paid $500,000 for your rental property. Its land fraction would be 0.30 x $500,000 = $150,000. By factoring out the land, your improvements portion would be [(1 - 0.30) x $500,000] = $350,000. The improvements are depreciable, whereas the land is not. Immediately, your maximum cost recovery potential is reduced significantly below your actual costs.

Segregating Improvements

The term "improvements" as used by your local assessor constitutes, supposedly, all improvements to land beyond that of its natural, pristine state. It is a collective term for all buildings, structures, storage sheds, sign posts, fencing, bulkheads, landscaping, driveways, recreational facilities, etc., physically on your property when assessed. No effort is made by the assessor — nor is he required — to segregate the improvements into different depreciable classes. The segregation is your job as the rental property owner.

There is a general disallowance rule (not expressly so stated in the tax code) on the segregation of improvements. If you acquire the property for an agreed lump-sum price (or some other bulk basis), and you fail to allocate the cost to each segregative improvement, you cannot depreciate any of the improvements separately. You treat them all as inherent components of the primary rental facility. When it comes time to replace an improvement separately, you can segregate at that time. You can do this because you have separate identifiable costs.

To sidestep the general disallowance rule, we offer this suggestion. Before ownership of your newly acquired property is recorded, have a professional appraiser allocate your total acquisition cost or other basis into logically separable categories of improvements. As an example in this regard, we provide you with Figure 2.3. Have the appraiser sign the allocated list of costs, and you and the seller (transferor) also sign it. Have the document included as part of your acquisition "settlement papers." A cost

```
┌──────────────────────────────────────────────────────┐
│         Letterhead of Real Estate Appraiser           │
├──────────────────────────────────────────────────────┤
│ Property  _____        Parcel No. _____    │
│ Address   _____                                  │
│                              Total Fair                │
│ Description _____      Market Value  ▶ $ [    ]  │
│ of Property _____                                │
│                              Date       _____    │
├──────────────────────────────────────────────────────┤
│           CERTIFICATION OF APPRAISAL                   │
├──────────────────────────────────────────────────────┤
│  I certify that I have examined the above described    │
│  property, and have appraised its fair market value    │
│  as follows:                                           │
│                                                        │
│     Land ( ____ Ac) ...................  $ 65,000      │
│     Building ( ____ Units)..............   130,000     │
│     Pool & pool house ..................    30,000     │
│     Landscaping, fencing, etc...........    15,000     │
│     Furniture, appliances, etc..........    10,000     │
│                                                        │
│       TOTAL MARKET VALUE ──▶  [ 250,000 ]              │
│                                                        │
│  These values are exclusive of all financing charges,  │
│  closing costs, and title fees.                        │
│                                                        │
│     Agreed to by:                   /s/                │
│                                 _____            │
│     ___/s/___ Buyer             R.E. Appraiser         │
│                                 State License No.      │
│     ___/s/___ Seller            _____            │
└──────────────────────────────────────────────────────┘
```

Fig. 2.3 - Sample Allocation of Purchase Price of Realty

breakdown of the type presented in Figure 2.3 is often accepted by the IRS for depreciation scheduling purposes.

Residential (dwelling) and nonresidential (workplace) buildings are set by subsection 168(c) at 27.5 and 39 years, respectively. All other improvements to your land must be based on the classification listings in Figure 2.1. You adopt the recovery period and depreciation method that seem most reasonable and realistic. But don't get too aggressive. You can't expect to be allowed to write off a new roof in three years, for example, when you know it will last 10 to 15 years or more.

When "Placed in Service"

The allowance for depreciation starts when a depreciable asset is placed in service. The depreciation allowance stops when it is taken out of service.

An asset is considered to be placed in service when it is in a condition of *readiness and availability* for its intended function. If in a state of "getting ready," it is not ready and available. Nor is it available, even if ready, if its use as rental property is not offered to the general public.

Example: You buy a 25-year-old 4-plex rental building in January. It is in general disrepair and needs extensive remodeling and renovations. It takes you six months to complete the work. In July, you place a "For Rent" sign conspicuously on your property. In September, your first tenant signs a rental agreement with you. When does depreciation start?

Answer: July, probably; but September is more likely.

It is possible that in July the property was not really ready. You were putting on the finishing touches and finalizing things, and wanted a little jump start on your depreciation deductions. Besides, what documentation do you have to support your July posting?

On the other hand, had you listed the property in July with an established rental agency, and entered into a commission contract, July would be your placement-in-service month, unequivocally. The presumption is that the rental agent would have seen to it that the property was ready and available, before spending his own money for advertising and screening prospective tenants.

Suppose you had a vacancy in one of the 4-plex units. Does depreciation stop at that time?

No. Not if it remains ready and available. Nor would it stop if you cleaned it and made minor repairs. But if you completely redid the vacant unit — painting, remodeling, improving — technically, it would not be ready and available during the refurbishing period. However, even if the effort lasted 30 to 90 days or so, depreciation would probably be allowed. After all, you are depreciating the building over 330 months (27.5 years x 12 months per year); what practical difference does a month or so make?

Depreciation ends when one of three situations occurs, namely:

1. The cumulative depreciation over the years (allowed or allowable) equals your cost recovery basis.

2. The property is sold, exchanged, transferred, or converted to personal use by family or relatives.
3. The property is abandoned, or withdrawn from the market while resolving legal, financial, or controversial issues.

"Allowed or Allowable" Explained

Another depreciation principle that has been long established is the *allowed or allowable* concept. This means that you cannot claim more depreciation than allowed, nor can you claim less depreciation than is allowable. In other words, you cannot adjust depreciation to match your income stream, nor to compensate for good years or bad years.

Pertinent to this concept is IRS Regulation 1.167(a)-10(a): *When depreciation deduction is allowable*. This regulation reads in significant part as—

> *A taxpayer should deduct the proper depreciation allowance each year and may not increase his depreciation allowances in later years by reason of his failure to deduct any depreciation allowance or of his action in deducting an allowance plainly inadequate under the known facts in prior years. The inadequacy of the depreciation allowance for property in prior years shall be determined on the basis of the allowable method of depreciation used by the taxpayer for such property or under the straight line method if no allowance has ever been claimed for such property.*

The gist of the above is that once you select an allowable depreciation method and recovery period, you have to stick with it ... to the end. You can't change the method or period without express written authority from the IRS. There is one exception. You can switch at any time from an "accelerated" method (200 DB or 150 DB) to straight line.

When acquiring and placing in service depreciable property, one's "gut reaction" is to claim the maximum up-front depreciation deduction possible. We caution against this, especially for rental realty and its improvements. With long-held property, there are too many unforeseens. There are too many tricky interpretations of the ACRS and MACRS rules. When in doubt, we suggest plain old-fashioned straight line depreciation all across the board.

Setting Up Your Schedules

Depreciation is not a one-year-only affair. It goes on year after year until your cost basis is recovered or you sell/exchange the property, or you abandon it as a rental. This means that you need to keep track of your allowed/allowable amounts cumulatively, as you go along. The only methodical way to do this is to set up and maintain a depreciation *schedule*.

Each rental property should have its own separate depreciation schedule. Here, the term "property" includes all types of improvements on each recorded parcel of land. For each property, you may — and probably will — have several subschedules. A "subschedule" is required for each property item (improvement) for which a separate depreciable basis can be established. A "depreciation schedule," therefore, consists of a primary schedule (such as for a residential building or a workplace building) plus one or more subschedules (for each separately depreciable item). If you have several rental properties, designate each set of schedules as Property A, Property B, Property C, and so on.

For reference purposes, each set of schedules should show an entry for **Land**. You claim no depreciation for land, of course. But by listing it as a separate item and showing its cost basis, it becomes self-evident that you have knowingly factored out the land. When your tax basis in land is not shown, the IRS invariably asks: "What portion of your total property is land? Have you included it (surreptitiously) in the depreciable basis of your separately listed recovery items?"

Once the land is clearly displayed on your depreciation schedules, you list each item of property for which a separate depreciation basis is established. You cannot, however, "componentize" a building (which you acquired as a single operating unit) by separating the wiring and plumbing, the roof, the heating system, the foundation, etc. When the need arises for replacing any of these items, you can then list them separately for depreciation purposes. You can then use a recovery period based on actual economic-life experience.

After the initial acquisition of your basic rental facility, whether or not you allocated as per Figure 2.3, you set up subschedules as you acquire and place in service additional items. If you refinance the property, for example, your total refinancing costs are separately displayed. If you have prior year suspended losses, these, too, can be separately displayed.

A proper depreciation schedule requires at least eight columnar entries — (a) through (h) — for each depreciable item. These columnar headings are shown in Figure 2.4. Also shown are three primary properties with separate example subschedule depreciation. Note that Column (d) is date of placement in service: *not* date of acquisition. Also note that Column (c) is basis for depreciation: not (necessarily) the full basis as in Column (b). When rental property is not 100% available to the public, such as being partially owner-occupied, the basis for depreciation is reduced proportionately.

If you set up your depreciation schedules conscientiously, Columns (b) and (e) — in Figure 2.4 — become a running cost history of your property. This is your "adjusted basis" from *day 1* to *day/year X* when you dispose of the property. At some point in time, all rental properties are sold, exchanged, transferred, or passed on to heirs. When this time comes, you want all pertinent cost records conveniently assembled.

Form 4562: Of Limited Use

For claiming the depreciation deductions on your tax return, IRS Form 4562: **Depreciation and Amortization** is available. The "amortization" applies to intangible assets, such as refinance fees, covenants not to compete, and leasehold agreements which are amortized uniformly over straight-line time.

For rental properties, Form 4562 is of very limited use. It is not designed for tracking cost history or prior-year cumulative depreciation taken. It is designed primarily for trade or business assets: workplace items such as machinery, equipment, computers, vehicles, tools, fixtures, devices, etc. The form is more concerned with business-use fractions for mixed personal/business items than it is for long-term investment in rental realty.

As matters now stand, Form 4562 is required only for the *placement-in-service year* of the rental realty depreciable items. If there is a year in which no depreciable items are placed in service, no Form 4562 is required. All of which means, as a property owner, that you have to do your own schedule-keeping along the lines of Figure 2.4.

Assets eligible for depreciation and placed in service during the taxable year are reported in Part II of Form 4562. Part II is titled: **MACRS Depreciation for Assets Placed in Service ONLY During Your Tax Year**. When you make an entry in Part II, you must also make an entry in Part III: Other Depreciation,

SUGGESTED COLUMNAR HEADINGS FOR DEPRECIATION SCHEDULE-KEEPING

(a) Description of Property items	(b) Acquisition cost or other basis	(c) Recovery basis for depreciation	(d) Date placed in service	(e) Depreciation allowed/allowable in prior years	(f) Method used; 200 DB, 150 DB, S/L	(g) Recovery period, years	(h) Deduction for depreciation this year
Prop. A: Single Family							
Land	$ 50,000	N/A					
Bldg. (age)	135,000	135,000			S/L	27.5	4,909
Furn. & Fix.	22,500	22,500			200 DB	7	6,428
Appliances	10,000	10,000			200 DB	5	4,000
Subtotals							
Prop. B: 4-plex: 1 owner occupied							
Land	86,500	N/A					
Bldg. (age)	168,260	126,187		Only 75% depreciable as 25% is owner occupied	S/L	27.5	4,589
Renovations	38,290	28,717			S/L	27.5	1,044
New Roof	20,000	15,000			150 DB	15	1,500
Pool, etc.	32,500	24,375			150 DB	20	1,828
Subtotals							
Prop. C: 10 retail shops							
Land	162,000	N/A					
Bldg. (age)	150,000	150,000			S/L	39	3,846
Reconstruct.	175,000	175,000			S/L	39	4,487
Refinance	35,000	35,000			S/L	30	1,167
Subtotals							

Fig. 2.4 - Example Depreciation Schedules for Selected Rental Properties

for items placed in service in prior years for which the depreciation deduction is continuing. An edited/abbreviated version of Parts II and III of Form 4562 is presented in Figure 2.5. Note that the Column marked "Date" is shaded out for the 3-, 5-, 7-, 10-, 15-, and 20-year items. This is because these items must generally use the half-year convention. Under this convention, the year of placement in service is important; the month and day are not. We regard Figure 2.5 as a short summary of those depreciation rules most applicable to rental property.

Repairs vs. Improvements

A thorny problem with depreciation schedules is the issue of repairs versus improvements. As you'll see in the next two chapters, repairs can be expensed. That is, they can be written off against your current year's rental income. Improvements, on the other hand, have to be depreciated and written off only partially against income, year after year. Most owners of rental property prefer to write off as much as possible "up front" and not stretch out the writeoffs over several years.

This is where the "allowed/allowable" mandate comes into play. After you have spent cash money on needed repairs, the IRS can — and often does — come on the scene several years later to say: "No; they're not repairs. They are improvements. You must depreciate them." This usually provokes an argument by the property owner.

What constitutes repairs versus improvements for depreciation purposes is a vast grey area of tax judgment. Much depends on the circumstances involved.

As a general guide, the term "repairs" refers to those expenditures for *restoring* an item of property to its original state or working order. That is, repairing is a restoration process only; it is not an extension process.

In contrast to repairs, improvements comprise three categories of property effort, namely:

1. That which *extends* the useful life of a property item beyond its original state or working condition.
2. That which *replaces* an original property item in its entirety, and

Form 4562	Depreciation and Amortization					
Part II	**FOR PLACEMENT-IN-SERVICE YEAR ONLY**					
Class	Date	Basis	Recovery Period	Convention	Method	Deduction
3-year	////					
5-year	////					
7-year	////					
10-year	////					
15-year	////					
20-year	////					
Residential			27.5 yrs	MM	S/L	
Non-residential			39 yrs	MM	S/L	
Part III	**OTHER DEPRECIATION AND SUMMARY**					
● Pre-1981 depreciation ⟶						
● Pre-1987 depreciation ⟶						
● Post-1986 depreciation ⟶						
					TOTAL ▶	

Fig. 2.5 - Rental Realty Entries on Form 4562

3. That which *adds to* or is tacked onto the original property item.

A good example of a Category 1 improvement is extensive renovations to property. In a residential rental, you repair and update the wiring and plumbing; replace glass; patch up the walls and floors; paint the rooms; repair the roof; remodel the kitchen, and so on. Taken as a whole, these are renovations (improvements) to property: not repairs. They must be depreciated.

Examples of Category 2 improvements are replacing an entire roof of a building, painting the entire inside *or* entire outside, replacing appliances with new ones, and so on. These replacements (improvements) also must be depreciated.

Examples of Category 3 improvements are adding a new room, converting a garage or storage area into a dwelling (or workplace) area, installing a swimming pool (or other recreational facility), building a new structure adjacent to an existing one, completely remodeling/reconstructing one or more areas, and so on. All of these additions (improvements) must be depreciated.

The general rule with respect to improvements to existing property is that the improvements are depreciated in the same manner (method, convention, and recovery period) as the underlying property items to which they relate. Any depreciation differences would depend on changes in the tax rules for the placement-in-service dates.

"Adjusted Basis" Explained

Our contention all along has been that good schedule-keeping of depreciation provides a current reading of your adjusted tax basis in each rental property that you own. Rental property is acquired primarily for the production of income. Consequently, it is not a capital asset that you acquire one year with the expectation of disposing of it the very next year. You probably would (should) hold it for a number of years. Therefore, if for no other reason than depreciation alone, your tax basis in the property will change over time. At any point in time, then, you will have an *adjusted basis* in your property.

If acquired through an arm's-length buy/sell transaction, one's initial basis in property is his cost: Section 1012. The term "cost" includes all expenditures necessary to acquire full legal title to the property up to and including its official recording. It is more than just purchase price. It includes **all** closing costs: loan fees, "points," title searches, appraisals, inspections, recordation, etc.

If the form of initial acquisition is by bequest (from a decedent) or by gift (from a donor), the basis rules are Sections 1014 and 1015, respectively. In essence, the basis of property acquired from a decedent is its fair market value at time of decedent's death. Property acquired from a donor takes on the donor's basis, plus title recording costs, plus any gift tax paid by the donor.

The basis of property acquired in an exchange is its carryover basis, plus exchange costs, plus cash or other property conveyed, plus any additional assumption of debt, less any money received and debt relieved: Section 1031(d).

Once property is acquired and placed in service as a rental, its initial basis will change. Improvements add to basis. They always do; that's what the term "improvements" means.

The principal subtraction from basis is depreciation. But there are other subtractions, too. Damage may occur to the property for which the owner is reimbursed by insurance. If the insurance proceeds exceed the restoration cost, the excess reimbursement is "return of capital" . . . which is a reduction in basis. If one dismantles, detaches, or partitions the property in some manner and sells/exchanges/disposes of the portion thereof — called "partial disposition" — that, too, is a reduction in basis (return of capital).

Altogether, the rules on adjustments to basis are found in Section 1016: *Adjustments to Basis*. Subsection (a) is the general rule for which there are **24** separate subrules. However, only about five of these subrules apply to rental property. The essence of these subrules is that you keep track of your additions and subtractions as you go along. You can do this directly on your depreciation schedules. Doing so, you automatically have an adjusted basis . . . at any point in time.

3

SCHEDULE E (FORM 1040)

For Rental Property Owners, Schedule E (Part I) Summarizes, Property By Property, All Income, Expenses, And Depreciation. For Each Property, You Must Answer "Yes" Or "No" To The Personal Use Question: 14 Days Or 10%, Whichever Greater. All Mortgage Interest Paid To Financial Institutions Has To Be Separately Totaled (From Forms 1098) For IRS's "Computer Matching." If You Have Qualified Mortgage Debt, You Are Not Subject To The At-Risk Rules, But You Are Subject To The Passive Loss Limitation Rules Requiring Form 8582. If You Rent Out More Than Three Properties, Additional Schedules E Are Required (Numbered Sequentially).

In the preceding chapter we explained why Form 4562 (Depreciation) is of limited use by rental property owners. Its required use is primarily for the placement-in-service year of acquired depreciable assets. If no such assets are acquired in a given year, the attachment of Form 4562 to the property owner's tax return is not required.

In contrast, Schedule E (Form 1040) is required every year that a property owner derives rental income. This schedule is a comprehensive summary of all income, expenses, *and depreciation* associated with each rental property. Furthermore, separate summary entries are required for each rental property separately. Each Schedule E attaches directly to your own Form 1040.

The Schedule E is titled: **Supplemental Income and Loss.**
If you have rented real estate before, you probably already are aware
of Schedule E. But there may be some nuances with which you
may not be fully familiar. These include certain headnotes and
footnotes, and tie-ins with other passive activities (partnerships, S
corporations, trusts). Schedule E applies to all ownership forms of
rental property: not just directly owned property. You can even use
Schedule E (for a short time) after a property owner dies.

One of the most important features of Schedule E is its passive
loss computations (via attachments) and display for carryover to
subsequent years. For this purpose, the official form is not as good
as it could be. Without a Schedule E for each year for each property
for which you show a net loss, there is much difficulty in
reconstructing your allocable losses, property by property, some 3,
5, 7, or more years later.

In this chapter, therefore, we want to overview Schedule E
(1040) and highlight those features which are not self-evident on the
form itself. Once you are adequately familiar with the form, it
becomes a useful permanent record of your rental activities, year
after year.

Overview of Page 1

Schedule E (Form 1040) consists of two full standard-size
pages, front and back. It consists of five parts as follows:

Part I — Income or Loss From Rentals and Royalties
Part II — Income or Loss From Partnerships and S
     Corporations
Part III — Income or Loss From Estates and Trusts
Part IV — Income or Loss From Real Estate Mortgage
     Conduits
Part V — Summary [of the above]

Part I is on page 1; Parts II through V are on page 2. For direct
owners of property (for which this book is primarily intended), page
1 of Schedule E is the dominant use. The entire page is devoted to
rental real estate. If you have no indirect ownership of realty (for
which page 2 is intended), you can bypass page 2, skip the Part V
summary, and enter your page 1 "bottom line" directly onto page 1
of your Form 1040.

The full official heading on page 1 of Schedule E is—

Supplemental Income and Loss

(From rents, royalties, partnerships, estates, trusts, REMICs, etc.)
▶ Attach to Form 1040 or Form 1041.
▶ See Instructions for Schedule E (Form 1040).

As listed above, Part I is titled: Income or Loss From Rentals and Royalties. The term "royalties" is often confusing; we should clear it up right now.

For purposes of Schedule E only, royalty income is that which is derived from natural resource land. Royalties are payments to the land owner by a lessee who extracts minerals, oil and gas, geothermal energy, sand and gravel, rock and granite, timber, coal, iron ore, etc. Royalties also may be received from copyrights and patents which you bought from someone else, and leased to a commercial producer. Royalty payments are based on the number of units produced (whatever the "units" may be). If land is your royalty-producing asset, you are allowed a *depletion* deduction for the extraction of resources. If a copyright or patent is your royalty-producing asset, you are allowed an *amortization* deduction for the diminution of its legal life. This is all we are going to tell you about royalty property in this book.

Thus, for our purposes, page 1 of Schedule E is for **rental** real estate only.

An edited/abbreviated version of an official Schedule E (1040) is presented in Figure 3.1. You need only glance at it, for now. You've probably seen it before — but you may not have. If you have your Schedules E prepared by computer, the computer printouts will not appear in any format similar to Figure 3.1. The same information will be monoprinted on two or three one-sided sheets of paper, with no typographic highlighting of any kind. So if your Schedules E are printed by computer, you may want to take an extra moment to study Figure 3.1.

The particular feature to note in Figure 3.1 is that it is set up to handle three properties: A, B, and C. This is the exact setup as it appears on the official form. The significance is that each property — A, B, or C — must be incomed, expensed, and depreciated separately from each other. A "separate property," recall, is each parcel of land for which there is a separate Assessor's Number assigned. The income, expense, and depreciation information for

Schedule E (Form 1040)	SUPPLEMENTAL INCOME AND LOSS			Year

Your Name: | Soc.Sec.No.

Part I Income or Loss From Rentals and Royalties

Caution: Your rental loss may be limited. See instructions.

Kind and location each property				yes	no
A	Personal Use? ●14 days or 10%		A		
B			B		
C			C		

● Rents ● Royalties	Properties			Totals
	A	B	C	
Gross Income ➤				
Expenses				
See Fig. 4.3 ➤				
Subtotal Expenses ➤				
Depreciation (See Instructions)				
Total Expenses ➤				
NET INCOME OR LOSS (subtract total expenses from gross income)				
Allowable Loss (from Form 8582)	< >	< >	< >	
Add net incomes from all properties ➤				
Add allowable losses from all properties ➤				< >
AGGREGATE NET INCOME OR LOSS ➤				

Fig. 3.1 - Edited/Abbreviated Version of Schedule E (Page I)

each property must be entered into a separate column of its own. That's why there are three property columns on Schedule E.

If you own more than three properties, what do you do?

You prepare additional Schedules E, and mark them consecutively as E-1 (for properties A, B, and C), E-2 (for properties D, E, and F), E-3 (for properties G, H, and I), and so on. When you use more than one Schedule E, you strike out the preprinted letters A, B, and C and re-letter them sequentially. Later in this chapter, we'll tell you about the totals column in Figure 3.1 when you have more than three properties.

You should note in Figure 3.1 that we have purposely avoided showing any of your deductible expense categories. We will tell you about these matters in the very next chapter. Meanwhile, we have more to tell you about the formatting arrangement of Schedule E, page 1.

Headnote Re Form 4835

In editing/abbreviating the official format of Schedule E, we suppressed one headnote in Figure 3.1. In the same space along with the Part I heading, there appears the cautionary statement:

*Note: Report farm rental income or loss from **Form 4835** on page 2* [of Schedule E].

Income from renting (or sharecropping) farm land is also rental real estate. However, there are significant income and expense differences, and differences in depreciation, that warrant a separate tax form for farm rentals. The Form 4835 is titled: **Farm Rental Income and Expenses.**

Because of the substantial differences between the Schedule E entries and those on Form 4835, we have set aside a separate chapter to discuss farmland rentals, namely: Chapter 8. Even so, we wanted you to know about this now, so that you can appreciate the versatility of Schedule E.

The instructions accompanying Schedule E tell you to use Form 4835 if—

(1)   *you received rental income based on crops or livestock produced by the tenant* [crop sharing], *and*

(2)   *you did not manage or operate the farm to any great extent* [absentee owner].

The instructions also tell you that if you prepare Form 4835, you are to report the *net* farm rental income or loss in Part V (Summary) of Schedule E. There, it combines with other net incomes or losses from Parts I through IV. You do not have to be an active farmer to use Form 4835. As long as you own the land and sharecrop it out to others to farm, you are in the rental real estate business.

Line 1: Description(s)

The very first line entry on Schedule E is "Line 1" — of course. The small preprinted instruction thereon says—

*Show the kind and location of each **rental property**.*

The accompanying instructions say—

Show the kind of property you rented out, for example, "brick duplex." Give the street address, city or town, and state. You do not have to give the ZIP code.

Line 1 is sublined into separate entry spaces for properties A, B, and C. We think you need to do more than what the official instructions say. Experience shows that IRS examiners will ask for more than just the street or rural address. They want to know how many dwelling units or nondwelling units are involved. They want to know your fractional ownership of each property listed. And they want to know how many months (in some cases, how many days) during the year each unit was rented. A dwelling unit is a house, apartment, condominium, mobile home, boat, or like property used for human living purposes. A nondwelling unit is office space, shop space, retail space, manufacturing space, sales office, and so on.

Our suggestion is that, accompanying the description for each property on Line 1, after the address, you show in abbreviated form the following information in sequence:

(a) Type of rental — use "R" for residential and "NR" for nonresidential, with each designation followed by the number of rental units, such as R-3 for triplex or NR-7 for 7 retail shops;

(b) Fraction of ownership — use "rounded" percentages, such as "65% owner" or "22% owner";

(c)   Months rented — show number of months, and fractions if other than 12 fully rented or fully available for rent, such as 6 mo or 8.5 mo.

If you are the 100% owner and you rent a property out for a full year, you need only show the type of rental such as R-3 or NR-7. If you are the 100% owner and the property is rented less than a full year, show the actual number of months rented. This is your disclosure that the property was either recently acquired, recently disposed of, or vacant for some reason.

If you are not the 100% owner, you should have in your rental file a copy of the title deed showing who the other co-owners are. You should be able to reconstruct your ownership percentage, should you be IRS challenged 3, 5, or more years later.

Line 2: Personal Use?

On Line 2 of Schedule E, you are asked the following question; read it carefully—

For each rental property listed on line 1, did you or your family use it for personal purposes for more than the greater of 14 days or 10% of the total days rented at fair rental value during the tax year? (See Instructions.)

Alongside of this question, there are the Yes-No check-boxes that we show in Figure 3.1. You must check "Yes" or "No" for each property: A, B, C, etc. You cannot leave these check-boxes blank. If you do, the IRS computer will jump-snap at you.

Before you check either box, the instructions say—

If you rented out a dwelling unit and also used it as a home during the year, you may not be able to deduct all the expenses for the rental part.

If the property is not a dwelling unit, check "No." [This is why we suggested above that you use the designation "NR" for nonresidential rentals. It is a tipoff that your "No" is perfectly correct.]

If the property is a dwelling unit, check "Yes" if you or your family used the unit for personal use....

What are "they" — the IRS — getting at?

They are getting at the personal-use disallowance rule. Specifically, tax code Section 262(a): ***Personal, Living, and Family Expenses***. This rule reads—

Except as otherwise expressly provided . . ., no deduction shall be allowed for personal, living, or family expenses.

Personal use of a dwelling unit is defined as any day, or any part of a day, that the unit was used by—

1. You for personal purposes.
2. Any co-owner who uses it for personal purposes.
3. Anyone in your family, or in your co-owner's family, except when rented at fair value.
4. Anyone under an agreement that lets you use some other unit.
5. Anyone who pays less than fair rental price for the unit.

Now you know why we suggested indicating your percentage of ownership as part of the description entry at Line 1. It is not just you and your family that they are getting at; it is also the co-owner and his family. In fact, if you let anyone — family, friend, or stranger — use the property without paying full rental value, your rental expense deductions are limited.

If you charge no rent for use of your property, you get no expense deductions at all. If you charge half-rent, you get only one-half of the expense deductions. If you charge no rent or partial rent, and want all of the rental expense deductions, including depreciation, you have to show "phantom income" to the extent of the fair rental value of the property.

The 14 Day or 10% Rule

The real meat in the personal-use question on Line 2 is *the greater of* rule: 14 days or 10% of the total days rented. First, you have to understand the question in order to know what they — the IRS again — are getting at.

Suppose you rented out a dwelling unit for 100 days of the year. You offer it for rent continuously, but there are no takers. It's in a resort area and therefore not likely to be rented out all 12 months of the year. So you decide to use it on weekends yourself or let other family members and friends use it on weekends. Suppose the personal use occupancy is 20 days: 10 weekends, 2 days each. What's the consequence?

In short, you rented the property out for 100 days, and you had personal use of it for 20 days. Oh, yes; we know. You worked on the property, repaired it and so forth. But, still, there was personal use of the property — either by you, your co-owners, or your family and friends — for more than the greater of 14 days or 10% of the actual rental days.

The bottom line result is that you only get to deduct 100/365ths of your otherwise deductible expenses and depreciation for the year. This is the "vacation home" rule which we are going to tell you more about in Chapter 6: Vacation Home Rentals.

If you checked "Yes" to the personal use question, and rented the property out to others for less than 15 days, you cannot deduct any rental expenses. You are allowed, however, to keep the 14 days' rent and pay no income tax on it. This is the "de minimis" rule for rental property [Sec. 280A(g)].

The message behind the personal-use question on Line 2 is quite clear. If you want to get 100% deductibility of all expenses and depreciation on your rental property, do not permit it to be personally used more than 14 days of the year. If this is your stand, then check "No" for each residential property that you list on Schedule E.

Depreciation Separately Entered

Let's glance back at Figure 3.1 for a moment. Look about 2/3rds the way down, at the entry which says: Depreciation (See Instructions). Note that this is a separate entry all by itself, after subtotaling all other operating-type expenses. Note also that it is a separate entry for each property.

The instructions regarding the separate line for depreciation tell you that—

The deduction does not apply to land and personal-use property.

This is your tipoff that if you use your rental property for personal, family, or friends' purposes, and you check "Yes" at the Line 2 check-box, the IRS will be looking for Form 4562: Depreciation. (Chapter 2 revisited.)

With respect to Form 4562, the Schedule E instructions tell you that—

You must complete and attach Form 4562 only if:
* (a) *You are claiming depreciation on property placed in service during* [the current year], *or*
* (b) *You are claiming depreciation on any property that is listed property (such as a car) regardless of when it is placed in service, or*
* (c) *You are claiming . . . amortization of costs that begins* [in the current year]. [Emphasis added.]

We've told you about placement-in-service assets in Chapter 2. But we haven't previously told you about "listed property" and "amortization of costs."

The tax term *listed property* has nothing to do with a realty broker listing your property for rent or for sale. For tax purposes, the term means "mixed-use" property. That is, property which is used partly for business and partly for nonbusiness. Although defined in excruciating detail in Section 280F(d)(4) of the IR code, the best definition is that contained in the Part V heading of Form 4562. This heading reads—

Listed Property — Automobiles, Certain Other Vehicles, Cellular Telephones, Computers, and Property Used for Entertainment, Recreation, or Amusement.

The point here is that listed property has to be separated into that which is used more than 50% in business, and that which is used less than 50% in business. Then you have to answer these two questions on Form 4562 (Part V):

1. Do you have evidence to support the business use claimed?
   ☐ Yes ☐ No
2. If "Yes," is the evidence written? ☐ Yes ☐ No

Next, you have to fill out a separate depreciation schedule for each item of listed property for which you are claiming depreciation.

As to "amortization of costs" with respect to rental property, these pertain to refinancing costs, litigation expenses regarding ownership title, reconstruction-period taxes and interest, and certain historical and low-income rehabilitation costs. There's a separate subschedule (Part VI) on Form 4562 for entering these costs.

Didn't we forewarn you that there's more to Schedule E than you probably realized? There's still more yet.

Footnote 1: Form 6198

For each separate property shown on Schedule E, you have to show its net income or net loss. This showing appears when you subtract the total expenses (operating plus depreciation) from the total rental income of that property. If there is a net loss, there is a footnote opposite the entry space(s) which reads—

If the result is a <loss>, see instructions to find out if you must file Form 6198.

Form 6198 is titled: **At-Risk Limitations.** This form provides opportunity for disclosing the amount of money, pledged nonrental property, and mortgage debt that you have "at risk" with respect to each rental property shown on Schedule E. This form follows the computational rules prescribed by Section 465: *Deductions Limited to Amount at Risk.* Thus, you may need a separate Form 6198 for each of your net loss properties.

The at-risk rules apply to rental real estate acquired *after* December 31, 1986. For the most part, these rules apply only in those situations where your acquired rental realty was "seller financed"; that is, in those situations where the prior owner took the mortgage note himself, rather than your going through an established financial institution or government-backed financing arrangement. You are **not** at risk to the extent of any seller financing. The prior seller may be at risk, but not you.

To illustrate, suppose you bought a $200,000 rental triplex. You put $10,000 down, and the former owner took back a mortgage note for $190,000. How much are you at risk?

$10,000 only. If you default on the $190,000 note, the former owner takes the property back, and you are out $10,000.

If your net operating loss on the above property is, say, $12,500 for the year, the maximum loss you could write off is $10,000. The unallowed $2,500 is a loss/loss. It remains so until you can show that you placed additional amounts at risk by adding more money, obtaining "qualified mortgage debt," or pledging nonrental property to the seller-financier.

Qualified mortgage debt — in tax jargon it is called "qualified nonrecourse financing" — is that which is obtained from persons and entities actively and regularly engaged in the business of lending money . . . or backing it. Qualified nonrecourse debt is that which is acquired from banks, savings and loan associations, credit unions, insurance companies, regulated investment firms, pension trusts, and government-backed lending guarantees. Included are family and related-person loans if the financing is substantially the same as that which is commercially available.

No qualified mortgagee is going to give a $190,000 mortgage on a $200,000 parcel of property (as in the seller-financing illustration above). Such a mortgagee would require a minimum of 20% down, or $40,000: *not* $10,000. Chances are, if the real estate market were depressed, the minimum cash down would be 30% or more. In any event, with qualified mortgage debt, your at-risk amount would be $200,000: your cash down plus your qualified mortgage. Therefore, the at-risk rules are only significant to rental real estate for seller-financed arrangements.

Footnote 2:   Form 8582

The at-risk rules are just the first loss-limitation hurdle that you have. There is one other hurdle. This is the passive loss limitation rule of Section 469: *Passive Activity Losses Limited.*

We introduced you to this item in Chapter 1, and we'll explore it in full in Chapter 5: Loss Limitations. For certain property owners, this is the primary tax impact of Schedule E. We just want to remind you of its importance at this point. All real estate rentals constitute passive activities, by definition.

The concern for passive loss limitations shows up on Schedule E at the line entry officially designated as: *Deductible rental loss.* (We show it in Figure 3.1 as Allowable Loss.) At the loss entry, this official wording appears:

*Caution: Your rental loss on line _____ may be limited. See instructions to find out if you must file **Form 8582**.*

The instructions tell you that, generally, deductible losses from passive activities are limited to the extent of your aggregate net income from those activities. There are certain exceptions for rental real estate, however.

You do not have to prepare and file Form 8582: **Passive Activity Loss Limitations**, if you meet ALL of the following conditions:

1. Rental real estate constitutes your only passive activity;
2. You do not have any prior year unallowed/carryover losses from passive activities;
3. You "actively managed" the rental real estate;
4. Your aggregate net loss from all rental properties is $25,000 or less ($12,500 or less if married filing separately); **and**
5. Your modified AGI is $100,000 or less ($50,000 or less if married filing separately).

If you do not meet all of the conditions above, you must complete and attach Form 8582 to your "totalizing" Schedule E. If you have more than one Schedule E, meaning more than three properties, your totalizing Schedule E is your last one in property sequence. Form 8582 aggregates all passive losses, after which the allowable losses must be allocated property by property. As we will depict separately in Chapter 5, each Schedule E has sufficient white space at the deductible loss line to record the cumulative loss carryovers for each property.

The "Totals" Column

The far-right-hand column on Schedule E (page 1) is labeled: **Totals**. This is not the total of every line entry on the form. Just certain key entries are totaled. Obviously, the gross income from all properties is grand totaled. So are the subtotals of all operating expenses and depreciation. Then there is a total of net incomes from positive properties, followed by totaling of the deductible losses from negative properties. All of this we depict in Figure 3.2.

Also in Figure 3.2 there is another grand total not mentioned above. This is the total that we have labeled: "Forms 1098." Form 1098 is titled: **Mortgage Interest Statement**. It is a special form prepared by banks and other financial institutions in the business of lending money for real estate purposes. The IRS requires all mortgage companies, to whom you pay interest, to report the amount of interest you paid. Because mortgage interest is usually the dominant expense item with realty holdings, the IRS wants to cross-check the interest information that you report on your Schedule E with that which your mortgage company reports. The

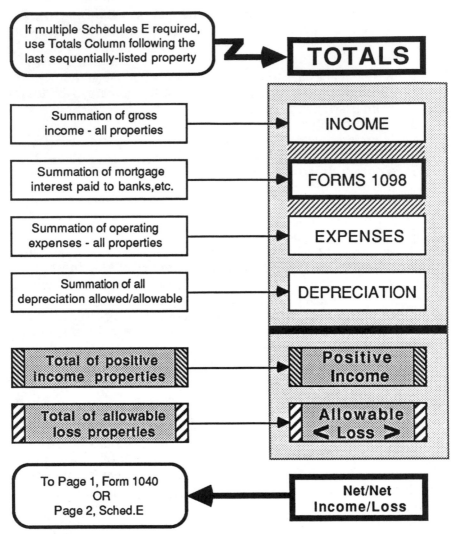

Fig. 3.2 - The "Totals" Column on Schedule E (Part I)

mortgage companies make mistakes in their reportings; the IRS makes mistakes in its computer-matching cross-checks; and you probably make mistakes as to which interest expense lines to use on Schedule E.

There are two interest expense lines on Schedule E (we'll discuss them more in Chapter 4). One line is for Form 1098 reporting; the second is "other interest" paid to those who are not 1098 reporters. There is much confusion here; yet the IRS makes no attempt to clarify or simplify matters. After you file your return, it takes the IRS 18 to 24 months to get around to cross-checking your 1098 interest entries. We are calling this to your attention so that you will strive more diligently to enter the proper grand total of the Forms 1098.

Suppose you have more than one Schedule E, say: E-1, E-2, and E-3. In this case, you leave the totals column blank on the E-1 and E-2 forms, and use only the totals column in the E-3 form. In other words, you do not subtotal each Schedule E when you have more than one. You use only the totals column in the very last Schedule E that you attach to your return. Otherwise you foul up the IRS computer, and the wrath of God will be down upon you.

As depicted in Figure 3.2, the very last line in the totals column on Schedule E is your net/net rental income or <loss> for the taxable year. If you are not using page 2 (back side) of Schedule E, you enter your net total directly onto page 1 of your Form 1040.

Summary of Page 2

For purposes of this book, our primary focus is on page 1 of Schedule E. Nevertheless, a quick summary of page 2 is in order so that you will have a complete picture of all variant types of rental activities. Whereas page 1 is designed for direct owners of rental property, page 2 is designed for *indirect* owners.

The distinction between direct and indirect ownership of property is one's fraction of capital investment in that property. In general, if you have contributed 10% or more of the total investment (in cash, other property, or mortgage debt), you are a direct owner. If your contribution of capital is less than 10%, you are an indirect owner. Most indirect ownership of rental property is in entity form, such as partnerships, S corporations, estates, trusts, and REMICs (Real Estate Mortgage Investment Conduits).

If you hold a REMIC interest, your prorata share of net income or loss is *not considered* as being derived from a passive activity. This means that you are not subject to the passive loss limitation rules. That is, there are no limitations on your loss writeoffs other than the amount of money and qualified debt that you have at risk. Your share of the REMIC income or loss is reported to you on a Schedule Q (Form 1066).

All other forms of indirect ownership of rental realty are subject to the passive loss limitation rules. These rules (for partnerships, S corporations, estates, and trusts) are considerably more difficult to comply with because of the complexity of reporting forms by the entity managers. Each indirect owner is informed of his or her prorata share of the net income or loss (of the entity) on such forms as:

Schedule K-1 (Form 1041)   — for estates and trusts
Schedule K-1 (Form 1065)   — for partnerships
Schedule K-1 (Form 1120S) — for S corporations

These "K-1s," as they are called, are messy and confusing tax forms with as many as 25 entry lines for pass-through information. Taxpayers having an interest in more than one entity have to combine several K-1s before computing their allowable losses for the year. Since investors are not permitted to attach the K-1s to their Schedules E, all K-1s — *plus* page 1 of Schedule E — have to be combined on Form 8582 before being transferred to page 2 of Schedule E.

Part V (Summary) on page 2 has a special entry line that we must call to your attention. It is the very last line on the page, titled: **Reconciliation for Real Estate Professionals**. The official instruction there reads:

*If you were a real estate professional, enter the net income or (loss) you reported **anywhere** on Form 1040 from all rental real estate activities in which you materially participated under the passive activity loss rules.*

If applicable, here's where you combine **all** of your real estate professional activities with your rental real estate activities, to take advantage of the Section 469(c)(7) exception to the otherwise maximum $25,000 loss allowed.

4

INCOME & EXPENSES

If You Have Multiple Properties And/Or Multiple Rental Units, You Need To Document Your Income In Ledger Form. Your Business Tenants, If Any, Will Report To The IRS The Rents Paid — Via Form 1099-MISC. There Are 14 Categories Of Operating Expenses Pre-printed On Schedule E (1040). Use These 14 Categories For Codifying Your Expenditures, Property By Property. Segregating Your Expenditures As You Go Along Will Simplify Your Year-End Summarizations For Schedule E. Loan Fees And Borrowing Costs Have To Be Amortized (Via Form 4562; Part VI) Over The "Legal Life" Of Your Financing Arrangements.

As a property owner, we assume that you are in the rental real estate business to make money over the long haul. You want some net cash out of your rental income from year to year and, from time to time, you want some capital gain on one or more of your properties that you may sell. Or, you may want to exchange your high-equity properties for high-value properties for building your nest egg, when phasing out at time of retirement. All along the way, you want an accurate accounting of your year-to-year "cash flow" activities. To a certain extent, this is what this chapter is all about.

Cash-flow accounting is where income and expenses come into play. In strict terminology, this means cash in and cash out. The cash in is normally thought of as income; the cash out is normally thought of as expenses. In a tax-accounting situation, however, income includes other than cash, and expenses — though certain cash outlays are made — are not all treated as expenses.

In addition to those cash receipts from your tenants, income also includes barter services, phantom income, vending machine receipts, security deposits, bank interest, creditor refunds, and other miscellaneous sources. In this chapter, we'll discuss the variations of income with respect to rental property, and the accounting self-discipline required by you.

In the case of expenses, certain expenditures — in cold cash outlays — may be tax treated as amortization or depreciation. These items are not currently expensed in full; they are "spread out." Therefore, all cash outlays do not automatically qualify as expenses. This is particularly true of capital improvements, renovations, title disputes, additions to, and refinancings of your property. The kinds of expenses that we will be dealing with in this chapter are more properly classed as *operating* expenses. These are those expenses necessary for maintaining the property in an ongoing state of readiness for rental use.

Variants of Income

Whether a tenant pays his/her/their/its rent with a check or green-paper cash, it is direct income. If a tenant is delinquent and owes you some rent, it is not income until you actually receive it. This does not mean that, at the end of the year, say, you can hold a check or cash and deposit it later, to count as income in the following year. It is income the moment it touches your hand, literally speaking. If you have an automatic-deposit arrangement, it is income the moment it is credited to your account, whether you see it, touch it, or not.

The same can be said of barter arrangements. Suppose one of your tenants is a plumber. He does some plumbing installations and repairs on your rented property (or on your personal residence or for some family member or friend). You discount his rent by some agreed amount. No money changes hands with respect to that amount. Under the barter-income rules, the dollar value of the services by which you reduced the rent is income. The dollar value of the services rendered to your rental property (only) is an expense. The plumbing services rendered to your personal residence, or to family members and friends, are *not* expenses incurred on your rental property.

What about cleaning deposits, security deposits, last-month's rent, and other tenant payments which are over and above the regular monthly rent?

You can treat these deposits as income, or you can treat them as not-income IF you set up a separate escrow-type trust account for such purpose. Unless you have a large number of tenants, where the deposit advances are substantial in amount, establishing a separate financial account, and allocating the interest to each tenant as it is earned, can add considerable complexity to your cash-accounting life.

If you treat your security deposits, etc. as income, when you refund any or all of the money it becomes an expense. It is designated as a "deposit refund."

Contrarily, if you have taken an expense deduction for, say, the payment of property taxes, liability insurance, utility hookups and, subsequently, you get a refund or credit adjustment, their refunds to you become tax-accountable income.

If you have multiple properties and multiple tenants, you may have installed various kinds of vending machines throughout your building(s). The most common of these are laundry machines, soap dispensers, candy and soft drink machines, and other convenience vending services. Since the income from these machines is associated with your rental property, it, too, is rental income.

Phantom income is the difference between the fair-rental value of your units and the amount of below-market rent you received or free rent that you have given. We are not talking about delinquent rent or skipped rent. We are talking about below-market-value rent where you voluntarily allowed some tenant to live or work in one or more of your units. The presumption is that these persons are family members, friends, or business associates. If you are conscientious about it, phantom income shows up as a "book entry" without any corresponding documentable cash.

If the location of your property is such that it is suitable (and legal) for outdoor advertising displays, and you allow some other business enterprise to advertise its products or services, the proceeds that you receive are also part of your rental income.

A summary depiction of the above and related income sources is presented in Figure 4.1. If you have only one rental unit, Figure 4.1 has little significance. But if you have 10, 20, 50, or more rental units, Figure 4.1 makes a lot of sense. It's a good check-list for the type of income ledger you should have.

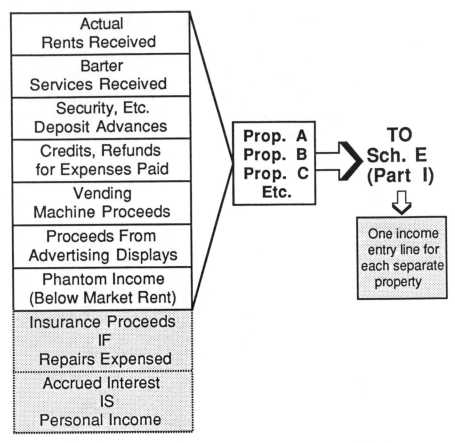

Fig. 4.1 - Variants of "Income" From Rental Realty

Separate Income Ledger

On the assumption that you have more than one rental unit, keeping track of your rents and rent-related income is an accounting chore all by itself. In the first place, you need some form of rental agreement that you and each tenant sign. The same applies to vending machine agreements, advertising display agreements, rent control ordinances (if any), and ongoing barter arrangements. In the rental business, you need something in writing in the event that landlord-tenant disputes arise. And they *will* arise. Count on it. We live in a very litigious society.

As if ordinary tenant litigiousness were not enough, there's always Big Brother looking over your income shoulder. The IRS wants to see a business-like ledger for keeping track of that income from your multiple rental units. If you have 10 units, say, you need to set up an account ledger showing the dates and amounts of your actual or constructive receipts from each unit. There are rental income accounting ledgers commercially available — or adaptable — for this purpose. We certainly urge that you obtain, prepare, and maintain a separate ledger for each separate property that you own.

Nothing satisfies an IRS examiner more than having a good income ledger, showing your attentiveness to the business at hand. Good income ledgers on rental property translate automatically into greater credibility for the operating expenditures that you claim.

The primary reason why income ledgering is so important is that not all tenants will be reporting to the IRS the amount of rent they paid you for the year. The IRS is gung-ho on computer tracking every dollar that changes hands in the U.S. . . . and eventually the world. But there are practical limits to its computer-matching paranoia.

Most residential tenants get no tax deduction for the personal living rent that they pay. So there is no requirement (yet) that they report their rental payments to the IRS. Business and commercial tenants, however, are allowed an expense deduction for the rents that they pay. To get this deduction on their tax returns, they are required to file a Form 1099-MISC (Rents) with the IRS.

Can't you see now the advantage of having an income ledger separating, as appropriate, the 1099 informers from the residential tenants? The rent information given to the IRS by your Form 1099 tenants will be cross-matched to that on your return. If there is no match, you could be computer hounded and harassed. To minimize this, be sure that your 1099 informants have your correct name, address, and social security number which appear on your own tax return. With a good income ledger, you should have peace of mind.

A schematic arrangement of what we are talking about at this point is presented in Figure 4.2. The rationale in Figure 4.2 is that when you prepare your Schedule(s) E (Form 1040), there is only one gross income figure associated with each separate property. If, somehow, the IRS learns or alleges a greater gross figure than you report, what backup evidence do you have to support your income entry for each property?

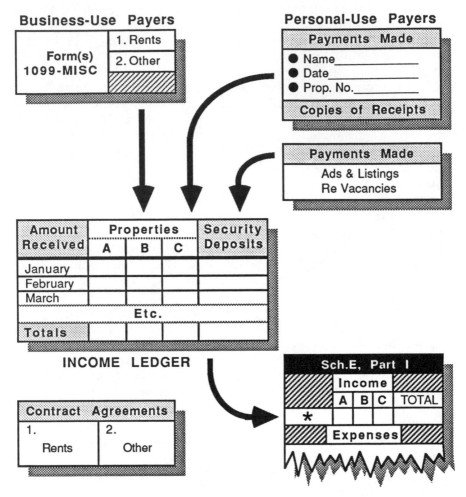

Fig. 4.2 - Functional Aspects of Income Ledgering

Separate Checking Account

One of the common tax mistakes of rental property owners is the commingling of their rental income and expenses with their other sources of income and expenses. The commingling is through a common checking account for depositing and expensing money, both personal and business. Those with one or two rental properties are most likely to do this.

Commingling of personal and business matters is a "No-No" in the tax accounting world. You must separate your rental business from your personal business. There is only one satisfactory way to do this. You need a separate checking-only account for your rental property activities. You need only one such account, even if you have several properties. Call it your "Schedule E Account."

Note that we stress *checking-only* type of account. This is to avoid any accrued interest being credited to your rental account.

As owner of the rental property and owner of the end-of-month or end-of-quarter balance of funds therewith, any interest earned on such funds is **not** rental or rent-related income. It is *personal* income. It would be reported to the IRS on Form 1099-INT which is quite unlike Form 1099-MISC for rents. The Form 1099-INT goes on Schedule B (1040): Interest and Dividend Income. It does NOT go on Schedule E (1040).

If you include the interest earned on your rental property account as rental income on Schedule E, the IRS computer will not see it on Schedule B where it belongs. You then expose yourself automatically to the IRS's computer-matching harassment. You don't need this.

So, take our advice, and use a checking-only, no-interest-bearing account for your rental properties. If it upsets you not earning the $10, $20, or so monthly interest, instruct your bank or other financial institution to "sweep" into a separate savings account all amounts in excess of a specified contingency balance.

If you have more than one rental property, we suggest that you get a commercial-type checkbook system. The stubs are sufficiently large enough to write in any payment description you need for your expense disbursals. After you read the following, you'll know why you'll need large checkbook stubs for codifying your expenses.

Overview of Expense Categories

Back in Figure 3.1, we presented an overview of Schedule E (Part I). At that time, we purposely omitted the various expense categories preprinted on the official forms. Now, we want to present these preprinted expense categories to you. We do so in Figure 4.3.

In Figure 4.3 we show all of the expense categories (only slightly edited) that appear on an official Schedule E (1040). Although sequentially line-numbered on the official form, the numbers we show in Figure 4.3 differ. We have skipped over the

RENTAL INCOME ▶			
EXPENSES: EACH PROPERTY ➤	A	B	C
1. Advertising			
2. Auto & travel			
3. Cleaning & maintenance			
4. Commissions			
5. Insurance			
6. Legal & professional fees			
7. Mortgage interest			
8. Other interest			
9. Repairs			
10. Supplies			
11. Taxes & licenses			
12. Utilities			
13. Wages & salaries			
14. Other (list)			
●			
●			
●			
●			
●			
SUBTOTAL EXPENSES ▶			

Fig. 4.3 - Preprinted Expense Categories on Schedule E (Part I)

first several line numbers in the heading and income portions of the official Schedule E, and started our numbering sequence at the very first expense category preprinted.

Note in Figure 4.3 that there are 14 preprinted expense categories. Categories 1 through 13 are functionally specific; Category 14 is for other expenses that you identify with handwritten notations. Choose your hand entries carefully. You should use the 13 preprinted categories if at all reasonably applicable. These 13 lines are what the IRS computer reads.

By showing 13 preprinted expense categories on Schedule E, the IRS is saying to you—

"You must allocate your rental expenses for each property into our designated categories, or we will disallow them as an expense. If your expenditures are truly rental-property related and they do not fit into the prescribed categories or into 'other (specify),' we will assign the expenses to your capital account for amortization or depreciation, as we deem appropriate."

This statement, of course, cannot be found in any official publication. Nevertheless, it is the actual position and stance taken by the IRS and its computer.

In other words, as a Schedule E filer, you have all the benefits and burdens of property ownership. One of these burdens is the proper allocation and codification of your expenditures to fit into the expense categories designated in Figure 4.3. This, indeed, is a bookkeeping irritant and chore — but you cannot escape it. In reality, once you get set up and organized, it is not as bad as it sounds. This is where that commercial checking account stub-book, mentioned above, comes in handy.

Codifying Your Expense Checks

By referencing Figure 4.3 or an official Schedule E itself, you can use the indicated numbers at each expense category for indexing or codifying your expenses. By using the designated category numbers you automatically key your expenditures into those expense categories that are IRS computer recognized. This should help you immensely when preparing your Schedule E return each year, property by property.

Unfortunately, if you use the official line numbers on Schedule E for one year, you may find that the following year, or some several years later, the IRS has rearranged Schedule E. It may either renumber or redesignate the intended expense categories. You won't know this until *after* your expensing year is over, when the new tax forms come out. It is for this reason, primarily, that we numbered the expense categories in Figure 4.3 in their alphabetical order, using number 1 for "Advertising" and so on.

To exemplify the coding system that we are getting at, suppose you have three separate rental properties: A, B, and C. With an income accounting ledger along the lines of Figures 4.1 and 4.2, when you make deposits in your checking-only account, you need not make any codifying distinctions between the properties and units from which the income came. Your income ledger does this for you, property by property.

But when you write checks to pay your operating expenses, you need to distinguish between the properties — not the units — to which they pertain. For example, you paid for janitorial services for Property A; you paid newspaper advertising for Property B; and you paid for basic utilities for Property C. On each payment check and on each corresponding check-stub, you enter such codifications as—

    Prop. A-3   (for cleaning)
    Prop. B-1   (for advertising)
    Prop. C-12 (for utilities)

If you will do the codifying on each expense payment check consistently throughout the year, you will find that preparing Schedule(s) E will be much simplified. Particularly so, if you have your own computer setup for collating and spreadsheeting the codified designations.

We urge you, of course, to pay all of your rental expenses by check, insofar as you can. If you pay any of your expenses by cash, we suggest that you prepare a cash receipt immediately thereafter and codify as above. This is where your own computer setup can be helpful.

Five Self-Evident Categories

Of the 13 preprinted expense categories in Figure 4.3, five are reasonably self-explanatory and self-evident. These are: (1) advertising, (3) cleaning and maintenance, (5) insurance, (10) supplies, and (12) utilities. We said "reasonably" self-evident; *not* "completely" self-evident. We want to add a few words to each of these five categories to clarify any uncertainties you might have.

"Advertising" (Category 1) consists of those expenses you incur for running newspaper "for rent" ads, for any public (legal) notices you are required to make, solicitation of repair and maintenance services, and the posting of "for rent" and similar signs on your own property. Advertising would also include a certain amount of promotional activities and give-aways (such as desk calendars, pencil sets, picture post-cards, business letterheads, etc.).

Advertising does *not* include goodwill contributions to local organizations and charitable causes. These are personal expenses, not rental.

"Cleaning and maintenance" (Category 3) includes those necessary expenditures for janitorial services, light gardening (such as cutting grass and raking leaves), and minor repairs (such as replacing locks, replacing broken glass, and touching up scratches and smears to walls). Cleaning of draperies and rugs, polishing floors, and removal of litter are the kinds of expenses in this category.

"Insurance" (Category 5) includes all insurance that you carry on the property itself — fire, theft, storm, earthquake, vandalism, etc. It does NOT include so-called "mortgage insurance." Mortgage insurance is nothing more than a variant form of life insurance on the property owner. It is not insurance against damage to property; it protects the mortgage lender only. If your property insurance is included in your condominium or association dues, it becomes a Category 5 item.

"Supplies" (Category 10) is a catchall for miscellaneous low-cost items, such as paint brushes, nails, one or two cans of touchup paint, small hand tools, wood for fireplaces, common area light bulbs, gardening fertilizer, small items of hardware, office supplies, business cards and stationery, and just odds-and-ends. The term "supplies" does *not include* substantial quantities of paint, lumber, glass, electrical parts, plumbing items, roofing material, or landscaping items. Such quantities must associate with and become part of the cost of repairs or improvements to the property.

"Utilities" (Category 12) consists of your payments to public utilities for water, gas, electricity, fuel oil (for common area heating), garbage pickup, trash removal, etc. It does not include telephone for tenants, as the customary practice is for tenants to pay their own phone bills. However, if you maintain a separate office devoted exclusively to your rental activities, an *allocable portion* of your own utilities, including your telephone, would be tax allowed.

Auto and Travel

"Auto and travel" (Category 2) is one expense matter where property owners often get carried away. They claim it when searching for new properties, visiting other property owners, attending investment seminars, and traveling to vacation resorts (domestic and foreign) to "look at" rental property. Our advice here is: Hold it! Your allowable auto and travel expense is quite limited.

Rental property is tax characterized as "Section 212" property: that which is **held** for the production of income. The expenses allowable against rental income are those which are "ordinary and necessary" with respect to *that* property . . . which is "held."

Section 212: *Expenses for Production of Income*, reads in full as—

> *In the case of an individual, there shall be allowed as a deduction all the ordinary and necessary expenses paid or incurred during the taxable year—*
> *(1) for the production or collection of income;*
> *(2) for the management, conservation, or maintenance of property held for the production of income; or*
> *(3) in connection with the determination, collection, or refund of any tax.*

The key point above is that allowable expenses are those which relate to rental property "being held." Expenditures relating to other property, prospective rental property, and attending seminars in far-away places will not fly. On this point, specifically, Section 274(h)(7) reads—

> *Seminars, etc. for section 212 purposes. No deduction shall be allowed under section 212 for expenses allocable to a convention, seminar, or similar meeting.*

So, now, what auto and travel expenses are you allowed?

In the first place, the term "auto" refers to local use of your auto on strictly rental property business. This means using your car for collecting rents, overseeing repairs, purchasing materials and supplies, and attending local property owner meetings and hearings (including attending tax audits and property tax disputes). For these activities, you should have some kind of business mileage log, to document the business use of your auto. You then expense at the standard (tax allowed) mileage rate, which is approximately 30¢ per mile. [This rate changes slightly each year.]

Secondly, the term "travel" means away from home overnight in pursuit of your rental property business. If all your property is local, you'd be allowed no travel-away expenses at all. But if you already held rental property in another city, state, or country, a limited amount of overnight travel would be allowed.

Certainly, traveling overnight once a year would be reasonable for renewing rental agreements, screening new tenants or a new property management firm, and physically inspecting the general condition of your property. One overnight stay would be normally sufficient. If your out-of-town property were severely damaged due to fire or natural disaster (hurricane, earthquake, etc.), several overnights' stay probably would be acceptable — if good cause could be shown.

Your "travel" expenses would consist of air and other transportation fares plus your lodging. Your travel meals would be questioned, but, if allowed, you would only get 50% of your costs. Any travel entertainment would be flatly disallowed.

Commissions and Fees

"Commissions" (Category 4) are those payments made to rental agencies, property management companies, or resident managers if self-employed on a commission basis. A "commission" is an agreed percentage of the rents collected. It may be 7%, 10%, 15%, or whatever. For this amount, the rental agent collects the money, accounts for it, disburses pre-agreed operating expenses, oversees maintenance and minor repairs, screens tenants, advertises when there are vacancies, and so on.

In some cases, the rent commissions are deducted from the rents received before any income is credited to the property owner's account. In such event, there would be no Schedule E deduction for the commissions paid. Paying rent commissions is most beneficial when property is owned out of town or out of state.

If, at some point, the rental property is sold, the *sales* commission is not deductible on Schedule E. Such a commission is a selling expense which affects the gain or loss computations on capital transactions.

"Fees" refers to "Legal and professional fees" (Category 6). These are property-related expenditures for attorney fees, accounting fees, tax preparation fees, appraisal fees, inspection fees, bookkeeping fees, and other fees paid to professionals who are engaged on an as-needed basis. With the exception of attorney fees, the services performed are usually self-evident in their relationship to the property being rented.

In the case of attorney fees, the payments must relate to the property *and/or* to the tenants thereof. The preparation of rental agreements, leasing contracts, eviction notices, and lawsuits against tenants and their visitors for willful damage to property are deductible Schedule E items. So, too, are legal fees for defending the property owner against allegations of local ordinance violations or misuse of the property.

Legal fees for title clearance, title controversies, title challenges, or title changes are part of the cost of the property itself. They are *not* Schedule E expense items. When property is offered for rent, it is presumed that the offerer thereof has proper legal title thereto.

Wages and Salaries

"Wages and salaries" (Category 13) is compensation paid to individuals performing services on your property on a regular basis, either full time or part time. If they work regularly for you throughout the year, they are automatically your employees. This makes you an employer. As such, you are required to obtain an Employer Identification Number (EIN) for use on all employee-related computer correspondence with the IRS (and with state and local agencies).

As an employer, you are required to make federal and state income tax withholdings, social security tax withholdings, and state disability insurance withholdings. In addition to these withholdings, you have to pay employer social security taxes, employer medicare taxes, and unemployment insurance taxes. You are required to file employer quarterly returns (federal and state) and pay your employer tax plus the employee withholdings.

If you have only a few properties, each with single-unit rentals, there is really no need for having employees. You do the managing, rent collections, and tenant screenings yourself, and engage independent contractors to do your maintenance repairs.

But if you own 10, 20, 50, or more rental units where turnover is extensive, your first employee-type preference would be a resident manager and resident maintenance person. Usually, a husband/wife combination living on the rental premises is ideal. You pay each spouse a salary or wage separately, and you furnish the dwelling unit free of charge. This is **not** a bartering arrangement. It is a salary plus lodging arrangement where the lodging is a *condition of the employment*.

On this very point, Section 119: *Meals or Lodging Furnished for Convenience of the Employer*, is applicable. While it is doubtful you'd be furnishing meals to your resident manager, it is customary practice to provide a dwelling unit. The rental value of the dwelling unit is *not* taxable income to said manager. In pertinent part, Section 119(a) reads—

> *There shall be excluded from gross income of an employee the value of any . . . lodging furnished to him, his spouse, or any of his dependents by or on behalf of his employer . . . if—*
> *(2) . . ., the employee is required to accept such lodging on the business premises of his employer as a condition of his employment.*

If you can possibly do so, it is best to avoid having employees. The employer tax liabilities and the quarterly computer harassment to which you are subjected can become unbearable.

Even a resident manager and spouse could be an independent contractor, if you paid on a commission basis and charged the couple your regular rent. In this case, however, you would need a carefully prepared independent contractor agreement signed by you and the manager and spouse in the presence of a notary. By being "carefully prepared" we mean that a clear, fixed percentage commission is paid on all rents collected, and that the manager and spouse have the choice of living elsewhere, should they so desire. You must charge them competitive rent with no discounts. Although the IRS would likely challenge such an arrangement, we believe your nonemployer position could stand up.

Taxes and Licenses

"Taxes and licenses" (Category 11), like all other Schedule E expenditure categories, is limited strictly to the rental property at hand. For this, the primary tax items are real estate taxes and special (local) district tax assessments. In some areas, tangible property taxes are imposed on nonrealty assets associated with the rental units, such as on vending machines, major appliances, and recreational items. In other areas, "severance" taxes are imposed for removing or recontouring the natural landscape, including trees and resources.

If you are an employer, employer taxes are also included in Category 11. This includes your share of the social security tax, medicare tax, and unemployment tax.

Property taxes on vacant land are not a rental expense, even if — someday — you intend to build rental units on it. However, if the vacant land is adjacent to your existing rentals, and you allow tenants to use the land for auto and truck parking, general storage, or recreation, the property taxes would be a proper Schedule E item.

In the case of sales taxes, utility taxes, gasoline taxes, excise taxes, and the like, these are part of the cost of materials, supplies, and other items that you purchase for use on the rental property. They are not deductible a second time.

Income taxes are never deductible on Schedule E. After all, it is the net income or loss from Schedule E to which regular income taxes apply.

Licenses are business licenses, rental licenses, permits, and the like for the privilege of renting property in a given area. This does *not* include vehicular licenses of any kind: auto, boat, or airplane. The expense deduction for licenses is limited to those mandatory requirements with respect to your rental property only.

By far the dominant allowable item in Category 11 is the real property taxes. You can deduct whatever you actually pay during a given year. This includes prepayments and delinquency payments. Most property taxes are payable in two installments during the assessment year.

Two Kinds of Interest

There are two kinds of interest deductible on Schedule E. There is "Mortgage interest" (Category 7) and "Other interest" (Category 8). We forewarned you in Chapter 3 about the IRS computer matching your mortgage interest data with that sent to it via Form 1098 by certain financial institutions. It is for computer-matching reasons that we identify Category 7 as "Form 1098 interest."

Not all mortgage companies and financial institutions report the interest paid to them on Forms 1098: **Mortgage Interest Statement**. Much depends on how each of your loans is characterized and structured by the lending institutions involved. If you have a pure first mortgage on the specific property which you are renting, chances are a Form 1098 will be issued. However, should a loan be characterized as a home-equity loan, improvement loan, or a second mortgage on property other than your rental(s), no

Form 1098 will be issued. Consequently, if you enter in Category 7 more than the Form 1098 reportings, you'll be deluged with computer-generated IRS tax demands and penalties.

On Form 1098 matters, the official instructions to Schedule E say—

> *If the recipient* [person or entity to whom you paid interest] *is not a financial institution or you did not receive a Form 1098 . . . from the recipient, report your deductible mortgage interest on line _____* [Category 8].

Category 8 (Other interest) includes non-1098 mortgage interest, interest paid to nonfinancial institutions, and interest paid to seller, family, or friends on borrowed money used in your rental activities. This category includes interest paid on borrowings for improvements, additions, major repairs, and refinancings. Also includible is interest on "accounts payable" with respect to materials, supplies, and services applicable to your rentals. Category 8 entries are not computer matched.

The IRS's computer mismatching problems are particularly severe when you co-own the property with someone other than your spouse. For example, suppose your proper ownership portion is 35%. Chances are Form 1098 will be issued in the name of the 65% owner with his social security number. The 65% owner gives you a copy of his Form 1098. What do you do?

The instructions tell you to report your share of the 1098 interest in Category 7. Then you are told—

> *Attach a statement to your return showing the name and address of the person who received Form 1098. In the left margin next to line_____* [Category 7], *write "See attached."*

We suggest that the attachment include a photocopy of the Form 1098 as issued. We also suggest that you instruct the mortgage company to include your name below the 65% owner's name on the Form 1098.

Repairs: Caution Required

"Repairs" (Category 9) is a touchy expense issue with the IRS. It is touchy because most rental property owners want to front-load this item with additions, improvements, renovations, and other substantial reconstruction efforts. Such efforts constitute capital improvements which should be depreciated rather than expensed.

In Chapter 2, where subheaded: Repairs vs. Improvements (on page 2-17), we forewarned you of this IRS touchiness. We described those types of repairs/improvements which must be depreciated. We realize, of course, that often there is no black or white distinction as to which is which.

As a rule of thumb — and only so — if expenditures for alleged repairs reach $1,000 or more *per rental unit* (**not** per rental property: some rental properties may have multiple units), you are cautioned to review carefully your characterization of the expenditures. In the truest sense, a "repair" is the restoration to an original condition when the unit was first rented. Example: You paint a white wall blue. That is a repair. But if you paper that wall or change its surface with decorative paneling, that's an improvement. You get the idea?

If your property has run down, has been vandalized, or has suffered fire or damage by a natural disaster, your restoration costs — regardless of dollar magnitude — may indeed be repairs. In this event, we suggest you take extensive photographs "before and after," and document the cause necessitating the repairs. With good-cause documentation, we suggest you organize your expense records into the following groupings:

Repairs — general
    " — carpentry
    " — electrical
    " — plumbing
    " — glass
    " — roofing

The "Repairs-general" should appear in Category 9. The other five (or other variant) groupings should be listed in Category 14 (Other expenses).

The "Other expenses (list)" is a catchall category for those items which do not fit into any of the other preprinted categories in Figure 4.3. Note that there are only five entry lines for Category 14 listings. Do not try to crowd more than five items into these lines. Surely, with some imagination, you can force-fit minor cost items into the preprinted designations.

5

LOSS LIMITATIONS

Rental Properties Sometimes Produce Net Operating Losses. When This Happens, Special Rules Limit The Allowable Deduction For Each Loss Property. The Unused Losses From One Year May Be Carried Over To One Or More Subsequent Years. There Are Two MUST USE Forms Which Supplement Your Schedule E, Namely: Form 6198 (At-Risk Limitations) And Form 8582 (Passive Activity Loss Limitations). Form 8582 Aggregates Income, Losses, And Carryovers For All Realty Activities And "Sorts Out" The Total Losses Allowed For The Current Year. When You Dispose Of Rental Property In A Fully Taxable Transaction, All Allocable Cumulative Unused Losses Are "Washed Out."

There are two loss limitation rules affecting rental real estate. Both have been mentioned — described — previously. They are Section 465 (At-Risk Limitations) and Section 469 (Passive Activity Loss Limitations) of the Internal Revenue Code.

With the exception of seller-financed mortgage arrangements, the at-risk limitations of Section 465 are not particularly significant to rental property owners. For seller-financed arrangements, the acquirer/buyer generally puts up a below-market amount of cash money, usually at the behest of the seller. The seller often wants to stretch the payments out for tax and income reasons. Thus, the primary risk is taken by the seller. If the acquirer defaults, the seller gets his property back without any legal recourse to the acquirer.

Although we have touched on Section 469 previously, we will touch on it again. It is one of the prominent cautionary footnotes on Schedule E for each loss situation that arises.

By far, we will devote most of this chapter to the Section 469 loss limitations. They affect virtually every rental property owner whose mortgage is not paid off, or not paid down sufficiently low to produce a net positive income. Mortgage interest is usually the dominant expense item on Schedule E. Consequently, except for qualified real estate professionals, property owners whose other-than-rental adjusted gross income exceeds $100,000 almost invariably face the loss limitation rules of Section 469. This means using another form attached to Schedule E.

The thrust here is not so much on the Section 469 rules themselves, as it is on the computation of the losses and keeping track of the unused loss carryforwards. Unfortunately, the IRS has not seen fit to adapt the Schedule E format to display — straightforwardly — your prior-year passive loss carryovers.

When Does "Loss" Occur?

At first glance, this seems to be a needless question: When does loss occur?

The short answer is that loss occurs when you properly show all income; when you properly claim all expenses; when you properly claim all depreciation; and when the net computational result is negative rather than positive.

Note that we have intentionally inserted the adverb "properly" *three* times in the sentence above. The income must be proper; the expenses must be proper; and the depreciation must be proper. This follows from the allowed/allowable concept where you are prohibited from juggling your income, expenses, or depreciation to avoid the loss limitation rules. That is, you cannot advance income or defer expenses and depreciation to produce a neutral or slightly positive income, thereby circumventing the loss rules.

Thus, a net loss occurs only after all proper entries have been made on your Schedule E, and the result is negative. The sum and substance of the "proper entries" for each rental property are as follows:

Step 1 — Summarize all income (including variants) for each given property.

Step 2 — List (in 14 categories) all operating expenses and subtotal.

Step 3 — Enter depreciation from separate computational schedule.

Step 4 — ADD Steps 2 and 3.

Step 5 — SUBTRACT Step 4 from Step 1.

If Step 5 is negative, you have a passive activity loss for that one property.

Repeat Steps 1 through 5 for each separate rental property and show its net income or net loss in the space provided on Schedule E (Part I). Do so, property by property.

Why "Property by Property"?

A "property" is a piece of real estate, consisting of one or more rental units, which is described, recorded, and assessed as a single parcel of realty. Single property status is not affected by the physical size of the land, its geographic location, or the number of rental units it contains.

Why is such a self-evident fact so important to us?

Because each single parcel of rental property carries its own operating income-expense records, and its own capital cost-depreciation records. Each property exists and must be tax accounted for, as though the taxpayer owned no other rental property of any kind. The fact that Schedule E accommodates three properties at a time (Figure 3.1) is a matter of summary convenience only. You cannot mix and commingle the tax accounting of one property with that of another. If you were permitted to do so, one could "juggle the books" among several properties to produce the most favorable tax results to the owner. Therefore, each property must tax rise or tax fall on its own.

The most immediate and necessary reason for property-by-property accounting is the at-risk rules themselves. In their most succinct form, the rules say that "any loss" from "an activity" (singular) shall be limited to the amount at risk "for such activity" (singular). Thus, obviously, only one property at a time is at-risk valued. Furthermore, any one property may be sold independently of all others.

Similar one-property-at-a-time wording exists in the passive loss rules. However, the at-risk rules apply *before* the passive loss rules can be applied. This priority of the at-risk limitations is clearly indicated on Schedule E by the sequence of the preprinted instructions thereon.

Because both the at-risk rules and passive-loss rules involve "suspended" and carryover/carryforward losses, there is a problem in tracking these losses, year after year, for multiple properties. This means that each property owner has to set up his own tracking system, property by property. There may be current-year losses, prior-year losses, and subsequent-year losses for which the tracking is needed.

A suggested setup for loss tracking where five properties (A, B, C, D, and E) are involved is presented in Figure 5.1. In most situations, not all five properties will produce operating net losses year after year. Nevertheless, the positive-income properties as well

Schedule E	Property-by-Property Summary				
ITEM	Properties				
	A	B	C	D	E
1 Income					
2 Expenses					
3 Depreciation					
4 Sum of 2 and 3					
5 Subtract 4 from 1 Income or <Loss>					
6 If <Loss> At-Risk Limits			Form 6198		
7 If <Loss> Passive Limits			Form 8582		
8 If <Loss> Amount Allowed					
9 If <Loss> Amount Unallowed					
10 Unallowed Prior Year(s)					
11 Loss Usable Next Year					
12 Disposition Gain/Loss					

Fig. 5.1 - Suggested Setup for Tracking Passive Losses

as the loss properties must be included in the tracking system, so long as all the properties are being held concurrently by the same owner.

The sole purpose of Figure 5.1 at this time is to point out the limitations of Schedule E for tracking your losses. Steps 1 through 7 in Figure 5.1 do appear — in different wording — directly on Schedule E. However, Steps 8 through 12 do *not* so appear. If you have one or more loss properties over a period of years, can you not see the accounting confusion down the line, if you depend solely on Schedule E?

At-Risk Form 6198

Section 465 addresses the at-risk rules which we have been referencing in general terms. We don't want to overfocus on these rules as they have little impact on rental properties which carry "qualified" nonrecourse mortgages. These are mortgages obtained through regular financial institutions which require substantial down payments in market-driven amounts, regularly amortized monthly payments, and competitive rates of interest. Still, we want to touch again on the highlights of Section 465 and particularly tell you about Form 6198: **At-Risk Limitations**.

What is indicated as Step 6 in Figure 5.1 appears on an official Schedule E (Part I) as follows:

Income or <loss> from rental properties. Subtract line _____ from line _____ (rents). If the result is a <loss>, see instructions to find out if you must file Form 6198.

The instructions tell you that—

*Generally, you are considered to be **at risk** for amounts borrowed for use in the activity if you are personally liable for repayment or if they are secured by property **not** used in the activity. You are also at risk for **qualified nonrecourse financing** by real property used in the holding of real property.*

***Qualified nonrecourse financing** is financing for which no one is personally liable for repayment and is . . . loaned or guaranteed by any Federal, state, or local government, or borrowed by you from . . . a person who actively and regularly* *engages in the business of lending money, such as a bank or savings and loan association.*

Amounts for which you are **not at risk** *include . . . loans from someone who has an interest in the activity* [such as seller financing arrangements].

The above instructions make no exceptions whatsoever for qualified real estate professionals owning rental property. Often, such persons are the very ones for whom the at-risk limitation rules of Section 465 are intended to apply. Professionals tend to engage in seller financings and other nonrecourse arrangements for minimizing the amount of money that they themselves actually invest in rental real estate activities. For these person particularly, the use of Form 6198 is a "must."

Form 6198 is confusing, to say the least. Its Part II, however, provides a simplified computational procedure which we depict in Figure 5.2. It is a takeoff from the depreciation schedules that we presented back in Figure 2.4 (on page 2-16).

Although Part II of Form 6198 is abridged, edited, and annotated in Figure 2.4, there are several features in it that you should note. First, there is your adjusted (cost or other) basis in each property at the beginning of the year. Your beginning basis is your previous year's ending depreciable basis *plus* your nondepreciable basis in the land. After all, the amount of money or basis you have in the land is also part of your investment risk.

If you have a seller-financing arrangement on your property, the balance of the unpaid loan principal at the beginning of the year is not your money that you have at risk. Therefore, it must be subtracted out. Any payment you make on principal during the year, however, together with any capital improvements that you make, add to your during-the-year basis adjustments.

Any depreciation allowable during the year, plus any other capital recoveries, decreases your end-of-year basis in the property. What is left, then, is the full actual amount of capital that you have at risk at the end of the year. Your deductible loss cannot exceed this amount.

Introduction to Form 8582

The footnote in Figure 5.2 is an abridged but unedited portion of the very last preprinted instruction on Form 6198. It tells you that if

Form 6198	At-Risk Limitations	Use separate form for each loss property

Description of property and applicable schedule: _____

Part II	Simplified Computation Using Basis in Property	
1	Adjusted basis, beginning of year [Include land]	
2	Principal balance, seller financing (if any)	< >
3	Re-adjusted basis: Subtract Step 2 from Step 1	
4	Increases during year [Additions,improvements, renovations, plus payments on principal]	
5	Basis before depreciation : Add Steps 3 and 4	
6	Depreciation (and other decreases) for the year	< >
7	**Amount At Risk:** Subtract Step 6 from Step 5 ▶	

Note: *If this loss is from a passive activity, get FORM 8582, Passive Activity Loss Limitations, to see if this loss is allowed .*

Fig. 5.2 - Property Owner's Computation of Amount At Risk

the loss is from a passive activity — which rental real estate is — you must go to Form 8582. This form enables you to determine how much of your loss is allowed in the current year.

Form 8582 is titled: **Passive Activity Loss Limitations**. This form requires aggregation of the individual net incomes and net losses of *all* rental properties that you own. If you have just one loss property among multiple properties, Form 8582 applies to all the properties. This is unlike Form 6198 which applies only to certain loss properties, one at a time. That is, Form 8582 is a multiple-property aggregation form, whereas Form 6198 is a single property form. Understanding this distinction will increase your comprehension of when Form 8582 is truly required.

The very last property-by-property entry on Schedule E reads as follows:

Deductible rental loss. **Caution:** *Your rental real estate loss on line _____ may be limited. See Instructions to find out if you must file* **Form 8582**.

The instructions to Form 8582 comprise approximately 16,000 words. They define key words and phrases, explain certain exceptions, and cite special rules that you need to know about.

For example, under **Activities that are Not Passive Activities**, the instructions say—

The following are not passive activities:

1. Trade or business activities in which you materially participated for the tax year.

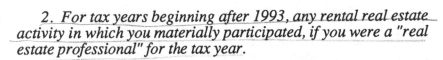

2. For tax years beginning after 1993, any rental real estate activity in which you materially participated, if you were a "real estate professional" for the tax year.

3. If an activity qualifies . . . above, but has a prior year unallowed loss [i.e., pre-1994], the prior year unallowed loss is treated as a loss from a former passive activity.

In other words, real estate professionals with no pre-1994 unallowed losses do not have to prepare Form 8582.

Otherwise, Form 8582 consists of three parts as follows:

Part I   — [Aggregate] Passive Activity Losses
                • Rental Real Estate Activities
                • All Other Passive Activities

Part II   — Special Allowance for Small Taxpayers
                • With Active Participation

Part III — [Aggregate] Passive Losses Allowed
                • Net income from Part I plus Part II

Note that we have inserted the word "aggregate" in the headings. This word does not appear on the official form, but it should.

Part I aggregates (totals) the net incomes and net losses for each of all rental properties that you have, regardless of when acquired. This includes any prior-year loss carryovers. Part II applies only to those who are not real estate professionals and whose total incomes are less than $150,000. Part III combines Parts I and II to establish your allowable loss for the current year. If the combined loss in

Part I is greater than that allowable in Part III, the difference is carried forward to the subsequent year (or years) . . . until used.

Exception 1 to Form 8582

The instructions to Form 8582 state very clearly that—

You do not have to file Form 8582 if you meet **Exception 1** *below.*

Exception 1 applies when you have in Part I an overall net **positive** amount, after combining all of your incomes and losses with any prior-year unallowed losses. After all, the purpose of Form 8582 is to compute your deductible passive activity losses for the year. If there are no combined net losses, the limitation rules of Section 469 (for passive activity losses) simply do not apply.

To illustrate Exception 1, let's postulate an example. You have five rental properties: A, B, C, D, and E. Assume that your current year property-by-property net incomes and net losses are as follows:

Prop. A — Net income: $3,260
Prop. B — Net loss: <5,620>
Prop. C — Net income: 8,470
Prop. D — Net loss: <7,290>
Prop. E — Net income: 4,850

All net incomes equal: 3,260 + 8,470 + 4,840   =   16,570
All net losses equal: <5,620> + <7,290>   =   <12,910>
                  The Combined Result   =   3,660

If you had no prior-year unallowed losses, no Form 8582 is required.

If your prior-year unallowed losses were <3,000>, Exception 1 would still apply. [3,660 + <3,000> = 660: a positive amount.]

If your prior-year unallowed losses were <4,000> instead of <3,000>, Exception 1 would **not** apply. [3,660 + <4,000> = <340>: a negative amount.]

The instructions further caution you that, for Exception 1 purposes, you cannot include in the aggregation process the incomes and losses from *nonpassive* activities. Nonpassive activities are sole proprietorships, general partnerships, regular corporations, portfolio investments, most capital transactions, and employment compensation.

Exception 2 to Form 8582

The instructions define Exception 2 as occurring when—

You actively participated in rental real estate activities . . . and you meet ALL of the following conditions:
(1)   *Rental real estate activities . . . were your only passive activities.*
(2)   *You have no prior year unallowed losses from these activities.*
(3)   *Your total loss from . . .* [all rentals] *was not more than $25,000 ($12,500 if married filing separately).*
(4)   *If you are married filing separately, you lived apart from your spouse all year.*
(5)   *Your modified adjusted gross income was not more than $100,000 ($50,000 if married filing separately).*
(6)   *You do not hold any interest in a rental real estate activity as a limited partner or as a beneficiary of an estate or trust.*

If you meet all six of the conditions above, no Form 8582 is required. All of your net rental losses are allowed, regardless of the number of properties you may hold. This means that any net/net losses from your Schedule E (Part I) can enter directly onto page 1 of Form 1040 to offset any other sources of positive income that you have.

The Exception 2 phrase "actively participated" is simply what any ordinary property owner does when managing his own property. It involves making management decisions, approving new tenants, deciding on rental terms, collecting the rent, arranging for capital improvements, and overseeing repairs, maintenance, janitorial, gardening, and similar services.

As you can see, qualifying for Exception 2 is a pretty tall order. The purpose of this exception is to protect the $25,000 special-loss allowance for "small taxpayers." This special allowance is authorized by Section 469(i): *$25,000 Offset for Rental Real Estate Activities*. Subsections 469(i)(3) and (5) address the phase-out of this special allowance. This is the role of Part II on Form 8582.

Statutory "Exception 3"

The new law enacted in 1993 effective for 1994 — namely: subsection 469(c)(2), (c)(7), and (i)(3)(E)(iv) — addresses qualified real estate persons. These are persons who—

1. devote more than 50% of their personal service time to real property trades or businesses,
2. perform more than 750 hours of *material participation* in such trades or businesses, AND
3. acquire and place in service rental real estate *after* December 31, 1993. [If such persons have prior acquired property, the passive loss rules do not apply after this date.]

Obviously, if a rental property owner meets all three of these conditions, no Form 8582 would be required. By exception to law, he would not be engaged in a passive activity.

Subsection 469(c)(2) defines a passive activity as including any rental activity—

> *. . . except as provided in paragraph (7).*

The reference to "paragraph (7)" is subsection 469(c)(7) which promulgates conditions 1, 2, and 3 above. The term "material participation" means—

> *. . . regular, continuous, and substantial.*

Subsection 469(i)(3)(E)(iv) addresses the phase-out of the $25,000 exemption from the passive loss general limitation rule of Section 469(a). In the computational aspects of this phase-out, a modified adjusted gross income is determined—

> *. . . without regard to . . . subsection (c)(7).*

This means that qualified real estate persons also get the special $25,000 offset allowance for rental real estate acquired *before* 1994.

The $25,000 Allowance

The $25,000 special loss allowance for rental property owners is not a fixed given. It phases out under certain conditions. There are filing status phase-out rules and, separately, gross income phase-out rules.

The filing status phase-out provisions are set forth in subsection 469(i)(5) of the tax code. This subsection specifically addresses: *Married individuals filing separately.* Under this subsection, two subrules apply:

One. The $25,000 amount is **cut in half** to $12,500 for each spouse, IF the spouses live apart for the entire year.
Two. The $25,000 amount is **reduced to zero** if the married-filing-separate spouses live in the same household at any time during the year.

The specific statutory wording in subsection 469(i)(5)(B) is—

Taxpayers not living apart. This subsection [re the $25,000 special allowance] *shall not apply to a taxpayer who—*
(i) is a married individual filing a separate return for any taxable year, and
(ii) does not live apart from his spouse at all times during such taxable year. [Emphasis added.]

It is not clear why married individuals filing separately are punished so severely. It probably has something to do with the "active participation" requirement for management of their rental property. Presumably, if they are not living apart the entire year, any acrimony between the filing-separate spouses distracts from, or interferes with, their property management decisions.

Subsections 469(i)(6)(A) and (D) define "active participation" as follows:

(A)   An individual shall not be treated as actively participating with respect to any interest in any rental real estate activity for any period if, at any time during such period, such interest (including any interest of the spouse of the individual) is less than 10 percent (by value) of all interests in such activity.

(D)   In determining whether a taxpayer actively participates, the participation of the spouse of the taxpayer shall be taken into account.

Thus, for spouses filing separately, the less than 10 percent participation rule could readily apply to one spouse or the other, to invalidate the entire $25,000 special loss allowance. Otherwise, single persons, divorced persons, and married filing jointly enjoy the full $25,000 allowance, subject only to the gross income phase-out of subsection 469(i)(3).

The Phase-Out Computation

The gross income phase-out of the $25,000 special loss allowance is determined computationally by means of Form 8582. The phase-out idea is that the maximum $25,000 offset is reduced 50 percent of the amount by which your *modified* AGI (adjusted gross income) exceeds $100,000. In the case only of married persons filing separately and living apart for the entire year, the phase-out reference amounts starts at $50,000: not $100,000.

The real catch to the phase-out computations is the meaning of the term "modified" AGI. Again, the rationale here is not clear. The only obvious modification required is the allowable passive losses themselves. Computationally, it is awkward (it requires reiterative calculations) to combine allowable losses in the same gross income figure which is used to phase out the loss allowances. Therefore, one's first step in ascertaining his modified AGI is to disregard all otherwise allowable passive activity losses. This makes sense.

One's regular, ordinary AGI is the very last entry line on page 1 of Form 1040. This official line reads:

*This is your **adjusted gross income**.*

This bottom line on page 1 of Form 1040 is your starting point for determining your modified AGI.

As to the modifications required, the instructions to Part II of Form 8582 say—

*To figure **modified adjusted gross income** . . ., combine all of the amounts you would enter if you were figuring adjusted gross income for your tax return except **do not take into account**:*

1. Passive income or loss included on Form 8582;

2. Rental real estate losses allowed under Section 469(c)(7) to real estate professionals (defined under **Activities that are Not Passive Activities**);
3. Any overall loss from a publicly traded partnership;
4. The taxable amount of social security and railroad retirement benefits;
5. The deduction allowed for IRA's and other qualified retirement plans;
6. The deduction allowed for one-half of self-employment taxes; **or**
7. The exclusion from income of interest from Series EE U.S. Savings Bonds used to pay higher education expenses.

Except for item 3 above, all other modifications *increase* your computational reference base — your modified AGI. The effect, of course, is to accelerate the phasing out of the $25,000 loss benefit.

At this point, now, we can present in Figure 5.3 our abbreviated and edited version of Part II of Form 8582. The computational steps shown are fairly self-evident. The asterisks (*s) call your attention to the married filing separate rules. That which we designate as Step 6 is your allowable loss amount based on filing status and gross income, as modified. This amount is entered in summary part of Form 8582 where it joins with the net income entries from Part I.

Computing the Aggregate Loss

Keep in mind that Form 8582 (Passive Activity Loss Limitations) establishes your aggregate total allowable loss for the year at issue. Your actual aggregate loss may be more than this amount, or it may be less than the Form 8582 amount. Nevertheless, the procedure is to establish your overall loss limit first, before allocating that loss to each loss property.

For our focus, let us assume that your only passive activities for the year are multiple rental properties. You have five of these properties, two with net incomes and three with net losses. The two net income properties produce $10,000; the three net loss properties produce <$15,000> negative. You have prior-year unallowed losses amounting to <$5,000>. Your modified AGI is $126,000. This means that your phase-out allowable loss is <$12,000> [150,000 − 126,000 = 24,000 x 50%]. What is your aggregate allowable loss for the year?

Form 8582	Passive Activity Loss Limitations				Year
Part II	**Rental Real Estate With Active Participation**				
1	Enter the SMALLER of the losses from Part I			$	
2	Enter $150,000		*	$	
3	Enter modified AGI	but not less than zero		$	
4	Subtract 3 from 2	but not less than zero		$	
5	Multiply Line 4 by 50%	Do not enter more than $25,000	*	$	
6	Enter the SMALLER of Step 1 or Step 5			$	
Enter amount of Step 6 into Part III					
	* See instructions for married filing separately				

Fig. 5.3 - Computation of the $25,000 Loss Phase Out

Answer: The aggregate allowable is <$22,000>. This is computed as: 10,000 income + <15,000> current-year loss + <5,000> prior-year carryover + <12,000> phase-out allowed. But, since your actual losses are only <$20,000> [the <15,000> + <5,000>], your current year writeoff is <$20,000>. You get no carryover benefit for the <$2,000> of unusable phase-out allowance.

Suppose, instead of <$15,000> in current-year losses, there were <$35,000> in said losses. For the otherwise same assumptions as above, what would your situation now be?

Answer: Your allowable loss writeoff would be the same <$22,000> as above [10,000 income + 12,000 phase-out allowance]. Since your actual losses are <$40,000> [<35,000> current-year + <5,000> prior-year carryover], you now have <$18,000> of unallowed loss [<40,000> − 22,000]. This <$18,000> unallowed loss can be carried over to one or more subsequent years.

Once you have $1 or more as a passive loss carryover, you have to allocate that loss to *each* of your loss properties.

The Pre-'94 Rules Remain

In the case of a qualified real estate person, the loss allowances and loss carryovers take on added complexity. For such a person, the rental losses for each property must be segregated into pre-'94 losses and post-'93 losses. This is because the rules on pre-'94 losses have not changed one iota. It is only the post-'93 losses for which the allowability rules have changed.

For example, consider that you indeed are a qualified real estate person. You have several pre-'94 rental properties, each of which produces a current-year loss. Assume that the aggregate loss for these properties is <$30,000>. Assume that you do not qualify for the phase-out allowance. You also have several post-'93 properties with an aggregate loss of <$35,000>. What is your tax writeoff situation?

Answer: Your <$35,000> in post-'93 losses is allowed in full [IRC Sec. 469(c)(2)]. Your <$30,000> in pre-'94 losses is unallowed. It must be carried over.

The 1994 rules limit your otherwise unlimited loss allowance to your post-'93 property acquisitions only. You cannot convert your pre-'94 losses to post-'93 losses . . . even if you are a qualified real estate person. We are certain that "anti-churning" regulations will be forthcoming to this effect. Your only conversion option is to dispose of each of your pre-'94 properties in a "fully taxable transaction." Clever property exchanges and wrap-around mortgage schemes will not work.

Conceivably, in the future, Form 8582 could be modified with checkbox questions for segregating the respective pre-'94, post-'93 properties. For example, we envision a subpart of Form 8582 being captioned—

Special Rule for Qualified Real Estate Persons

This subpart would then ask such checkbox questions as:

1. Was more than 50% of your personal service time performed in real estate trades or businesses? ☐ Yes ☐ No
2. If "Yes," did you perform more than 750 hours of material participation in such trades or businesses? ☐ Yes ☐ No
3. If "Yes," did you acquire and place in service rental real estate after December 31, 1993? ☐ Yes ☐ No

4. If "Yes," did your rental real estate activities result in a net loss in 1994 (and thereafter)?   ☐ Yes ☐ No

5. If "Yes," enter here (and in Part IV below) the amount of such qualified rental real estate loss ▶ ▶ ▶ $_____

If you answer "No" to any of the above questions, do not complete this part of the form. You do not qualify for the special real estate professional exclusion.

Allocating the Allowable Loss

Let's take a simple situation in which you have five pre-'94 rental loss properties (current-year) as follows:

Property A — <3,500>
Property B — <2,800>
Property C — <6,200>
Property D — <4,300>
Property E — <u><8,200></u>
           <$25,000>

Assume that there is a <$5,000> prior-year unallowed loss which is carried over to the current year. Also, assume that your modified AGI is $126,000. What are your allowable losses for the year, and how do you allocate the deductible amount to each of the five loss properties above?

Your allowable loss is simply the phase-out allowable amount which is <$12,000>. This is the same figure that we computed earlier for a modified AGI of $126,000.

Your actual total losses for the year are <$30,000> [<25,000 current-year + <5,000> prior-year carryover]. Thus, you have an unallowed loss of <$18,000> [<30,000> - <12,000>] which is carried forward to the following year. How is the <$12,000> allowable aggregate loss allocated to the five properties above?

The <$12,000> is allocated in proportion to the fractional ratio that each property contributes to the total current losses for the year. We do this fractional allocation for you in Figure 5.4. Column (d) represents the allocated amounts deductible in the current year. Column (f) represents the aggregated carryovers to the subsequent year . . . or years.

Supplement to Form 8582		Aggregate Losses Allowed : <$12,000> Unallowed Losses Carried Over : <$18,000>			
(a) Property	(b) Current Losses	(c) Ratio	(d) Current Allocation	(e) Current Unallowed	(f) Allocated Carryovers
A	$3,500	0.140	1,680	1,820	2,520
B	2,800	0.112	1,344	1,456	2,016
C	6,200	0.248	2,976	3,224	4,464
D	4,300	0.172	2,064	2,236	3,096
E	8,200	0.328	3,936	4,264	5,904
TOTAL	25,000	1.000	12,000	13,000	18,000

Fig. 5.4 - Example Allocation of Form 8582 Loss Allowed

Treatment of the Carryovers

When there are unallowed losses in the current year, and prior-year unallowed losses, the cumulative unalloweds are carried forward to the next taxable year. This is the statutory gist of subsection 469(b), to wit—

Except as otherwise provided in this section [Sec. 469 of the tax code]*, any loss . . . from an activity which is disallowed under subsection (a) shall be treated as a deduction . . . **allocable to such activity** in the next taxable year.* [Emphasis added.]

Carefully note the phrase: "allocable to such activity." This allocation includes both the current-year and prior-year unalloweds. This is what we exemplified in Column (f) of Figure 5.4.

The problem with all passive loss carryovers is tracking and allocating these losses year after year. One or two activities with one or two loss years is not difficult to track. You can do it in your head. But if you have five properties, with multiple net losses over a five-year period, for example, you face a tracking/allocation nightmare.

We tried to forewarn you of this nightmare back in Figure 5.1. That figure represents just one suggested way for your tracking setup. Another suggested way is to use the backside of Form 8582 and prepare your own tabulations as we have done in Figure 5.4.

The backside of an official Form 8582 is blank. This blank side provides ample room for your own carryover columnar arrangements.

Why is keeping track of your carryover passive losses so important?

There are three reasons—

One. The carryover losses are not disallowed totally; they are only disallowed currently. Only your own record-keeping inattention will cause their total disallowance.

Two. In some subsequent year, one or more of your loss properties may produce net income instead of net loss. At that time, your respective carryover allocations can be used as offsets against that income.

Three. In some subsequent year, one or more of your loss properties may be sold. At that time, your respective carryover allocations can be used to offset any capital gain on each sale. Thus, in the ultimate, your carryover passive losses become a built-in tax shelter for strategic dispositions of your properties.

Disposition Accounting

Sooner or later, an owner of multiple rental properties will dispose of one or more of his properties. If he does so in an arm's-length (fully taxable) transaction, all of the suspended losses allocable to the property disposed of can be washed out. They are tax recognized in full in the year of disposition. The manner of doing so depends on whether a net gain or a net loss results from the disposition transaction.

If a tax-accountable gain derives from the transaction in and of itself, the gain is treated as passive activity gross income. As such, it adds to all other passive activity net incomes for readjusting the loss allocations among the loss properties not disposed of. To qualify for this passive income treatment, the dispositional gain must derive from property which has been used as rental property for (a) at least 20 percent of the total time held, or (b) the entire 24-month period ending on the date of disposition.

To illustrate the tax accounting advantage of a dispositional gain, consider five properties with an aggregate passive loss of

<$30,000>: current year plus prior year unallowed. If just *one* of those properties were sold with a net $30,000 capital gain, that one disposition alone would offset all of the cumulative passive losses. Therefore, all losses allocable to each property would be allowed on Schedule E (Part I). The net disposition gain, however, would go on Schedule D (1040): Capital Gains and Losses.

In the case of capital loss upon disposition of a rental property, a special recharacterization rule comes into play. This rule — subsection 469(g)(1)(A) — converts the disposition loss to a *nonpassive* loss which can be used to offset any nonpassive income. To determine the amount of this nonpassive loss, however, you must first use Form 8582 to determine the amount allocable to the property sold. This is similar to what we did in Figure 5.4 with the difference being an additional allowable current-year loss. Because nonpassive losses *reduce* your modified AGI, the increased loss would allow you to take fuller advantage of the $25,000 special loss allowance.

If the disposition loss is greater than the otherwise unused portion of the $25,000 special loss allowance, the excess loss is entered on **Form 4797**: Sales of Business Property. On Form 4797, the excess loss is treated as nonpassive (ordinary) loss which, by following the instructions on the form, leads you to a special line on page 1 of your Form 1040: *Other gains or <losses>; attach Form 4797.* Once on page 1 of Form 1040, your excess disposition loss combines with other positive sources of income for beneficial tax offsetting.

6

VACATION HOME RENTALS

If You Own A Vacation Home, A Second Home, Or Rent Rooms In Your Personal Residence, The "Vacation Home" Rental Rules Apply. The Rules Segregate All Of Your Property Expenses Into Three Classes: I (Taxes & Interest), II (Operating Expenses), and III (Depreciation). You Apply To Each Class An AER Factor: APPLICABLE EXPENSE RATIO. This Is Your "Fair Rental Days" Divided By Your Total Use Days (Personal Plus Rental) For The Year. The Rules Prevent You From Claiming Any Net Rental Loss. However, Your Unallowed Losses Can Be Carried Over To Subsequent Years Until the Property Is Sold Or Listed For A "Qualified Rental Period."

A "vacation home" typically is one's second home in an area generally considered desirable for recreation purposes. It may be a cabin in the mountains, a houseboat on a lake, a cottage at the seashore, or a condo in an established resort area. It may also be a genuine second home in a metropolitan area closer to one's place of work than his principal residence.

The term "vacation/second" home implies that the property was acquired for the pleasure and convenience of the owner, rather than as a profit-seeking, income-producing realty asset. A vacation or second residence also implies that it is customarily vacant most of the year. The owner may rent it out during a portion of the year to help defray its cost and upkeep, in which case stringent and special tax rules apply. These rules are the focus and thrust of this chapter.

In synopsis form, the vacation home rental rules say that you must allocate all expenses and depreciation in direct proportion to the number of days actually rented during the year. The rules also provide that the directly-allocable expenses cannot exceed your actual fair rental income.

The vacation home rules also apply to renting out one or more rooms of your regular residence, if you have no second home. Renting rooms in your principal residence is tax treated as having two properties: one being your own residence, the second being the rented portion of your residence.

The vacation home rules also apply to mobile homes, motor homes, campers, trailers, boats, and any other structure equipped with plumbing, kitchen, sleeping facilities, and a living area. The fact that a structure can be moved, or is a means of transportation, does not prevent its classification as a "dwelling unit" for the vacation rental rules.

The "Trigger" Question

It appears as Line 2 on Schedule E, Part I. The trigger question is—

For each property listed on line 1, did you or your family use it for personal purposes for more than the greater of 14 days or 10% of the total days rented at fair rental value during the tax year? ☐ *Yes* ☐ *No.*

If you answer "Yes," you trigger all of the vacation home rules of **Section 280A** before entering any of your expense deductions on Schedule E.

If you answer "No," the presumption is that the property you describe is indeed bona fide rental income realty. Your "No" means that it is not your vacation home; it is not your second home; nor is it your primary residence where you are renting rooms to others.

If you answer "Yes" to the trigger question, you are not prohibited totally from claiming your allocable rental expenses. A "Yes" simply limits the kind of expenses that you can claim, and the overall amount that you can claim. So, claim all of your proper expenses even if you do answer "Yes."

Why 14 days? Why not 15, 20, or some other number?

Because 14 days is two weeks. Two weeks is the average length of a paid vacation for most U.S. taxpayers. If one buys a dwelling unit for purely vacation reasons, he certainly wants to enjoy personal use of that property for at least 14 days of the year. Hence, the tax characterization: vacation home rental rules.

A "day" for vacation rule tax purposes is not necessarily a full 24-hour day. It is *any part* of a day for which the indicated property is used for personal purposes. Using for personal purposes means eating there, sleeping there, or entertaining there for as little as one hour of a day. It excludes eating box lunches and using toilet facilities while there on a bona fide repair and maintenance visit. Sleeping there overnight while on a maintenance visit would constitute personal use. Working there but sleeping elsewhere would not constitute a personal-use day.

The trigger question phrase "you or your family" includes also certain nonfamily persons. A nonfamily person is any person or entity with an ownership interest in the property, or who has an interest in other like-kind property where you or your family can trade vacation stays.

The 10% part of the trigger question is to preempt against your letting family, friends, and others use the alleged rental property free of charge, or at a fee below its fair rental market value. The 10% relates to the number of fair rental days actually rented during the taxable year.

A "fair rental day" is the rental amount which the dwelling unit would rent to the general public under competitive market conditions. A fair rental value in the summertime could well differ from that in the wintertime.

Overview of Section 280A

The genesis of the vacation home rules appears in Section 280A of the Internal Revenue Code. It comprises approximately 2,000 words of tax law, organized into approximately 20 subsections. There are, of course, additional words in many IRS regulations. However, for our purposes, the law itself is sufficiently clear. As such, the pertinent subsections are presented in Figure 6.1.

Carefully note in Figure 6.1 that the official heading to Section 280A is—

Disallowance of Certain Expenses in Connection With Business Use of Home, Rental of Vacation Homes, Etc.

INTERNAL REVENUE CODE	
Chapter 1	Normal Taxes and Surtaxes
Subchapter B	Computation of Taxable Income
Part IX	Items Not Deductible

Sec. 280 A	Disallowance of Certain Expenses in Connection With Business Use of Home, Rental of Vacation Homes, Etc.	
Subsection		Heading & Subheading
(a)		General Rule
(b)		Exception for Interest, Taxes, Casualty Losses
(c)		Exceptions for Certain Business or Rental Use
	(1)	Certain Business Use
	(2)	Certain Storage Use
	(3)	Rental Use
	(4)	Use in Providing Day Care Services
	(5)	Limitations on Deductions
	(6)	Treatment of Rental to Employer
(d)		Use as Residence
	(1)	In General
	(2)	Personal Use of Unit
	(3)	Rental to Family Member, Etc.
	(4)	Rental of Principal Residence
(e)		Expenses Attributable to Rental
	(1)	In General
	(2)	Exception for Deductions Otherwise Allowable
(f)		Definitions and Special Rules
	(1)	Dwelling Unit Defined
	(2)	Personal Use by Shareholders of S Corporation
	(3)	Coordination With Section 183
	(4)	Coordination With Section 162 (a)(2)
(g)		Special Rule for Certain Rental Use
	(1)	Rented for Less Than 15 Days
	(2)	Proceeds Excluded from Gross Income

Fig. 6.1 - Detailed Outline of Contents of Section 280 A

This heading alone covers a lot of statutory ground. The "etc." refers to its definition of a dwelling unit, family use, fair rental value, and coordination with other sections of the tax code.

Section 280A does not stand alone. Its interpretation must be coordinated with other sections of tax law. The three most pertinent coordinating sections are—

1. Section 162: Trade or Business Expenses
   — hence reference to "business use of home" in the official heading;
2. Section 183: Activities Not Engaged in For Profit
   — hence reference to "disallowance of certain expenses" in the official heading; and
3. Section 212: Expense for Production of Income
   — hence reference to "rental of vacation homes" in the official heading.

The general principles in each of these referencing sections are the same. If you incur appropriate expenses in producing tax accountable income, the expenses are allowed at least to the extent of your income. They are allowed, provided there is a profit motive in seeking the income. When the profit motive is lacking, expenses can never exceed income. But where the profit motive is clear-cut, expenses may actually exceed income, thus producing a net loss for the year.

In short, the vacation home rental rules of Section 280A derive from the IRS's version of profit motive concepts. The IRS premise is that you acquired your vacation/second home primarily for personal reasons: not for business/rental reasons. Therefore, Section 280A is designed to eliminate any tax benefits where the perceived motive for renting a home is the reduction of personal (operating) expenses and not the long-term realization of profit.

General Disallowance, With Exceptions

The overall thrust of Section 280A is to disallow all business/rental expenses in connection with one's personal residence (primary home, second home, vacation home) . . . *except as otherwise provided.* This general disallowance principle is set forth harshly in subsection (a).

Subsection (a) of 280A: *General Rule* reads as—

Except as otherwise provided in this section, in the case of a taxpayer who is an individual . . ., no deduction otherwise allowable under this chapter shall be allowed with respect to the use of a dwelling unit which is used by the taxpayer during the year as a residence.

Suppose you read no further than subsection (a) above. You are immediately put on notice that if you use a dwelling unit (vacation home or other) as a personal residence at any time during the year, no expenses of any kind are allowed. This is the impact of the general rule of disallowance. This is broad and all-sweeping.

Fortunately, there is an escape hatch. The very opening phrase of subsection (a) says—

Except as otherwise provided in this section . . .

. . . meaning Section 280A. In other words, the exceptions to the general disallowance rule with respect to vacation home rentals can be found only in Section 280A itself.

The foremost exception in 280A is its subsection (b). This subsection reads in full as follows:

(b) ***Exception for Interest, Taxes, Casualty Losses, Etc.***
Subsection (a) shall not apply to any deduction allowable to the taxpayer without regard to its connection with his trade or business (or with his income-producing activity).

This subsection (b) wording by itself is fuzzy and ambiguous. Its heading is more specific. It directs your attention to "interest, taxes, casualty losses, etc." (such as contributions). These are statutory allowances known as *itemized deductions* which are available to all individuals, whether using or renting a personal residence or not.

The exception for "interest" refers to *qualified residence interest* which is defined in Code Section 163(h)(3). Subsection 163(a) therewith says that—

There shall be allowed as a deduction all interest paid or accrued within the taxable year on indebtedness.

The same "shall be allowed as a deduction" applies to property taxes [Sec. 164(a)(1)], casualty losses [Sec. 165(h)(2)], charitable, etc., contributions and gifts [Sec. 170(a)(1)], and other statutory allowances for personal items. The point in subsection (b) is that Section 280A(a) is not intended to block out those deductions which are otherwise allowable with respect to home ownership. Section 280A(a), general disallowance, applies expressly to operating-type expenses (insurance, repairs, utilities, depreciation, etc.) when renting any form of a personal residence.

De Minimis Rental Use

Another exception to subsection (a) of 280A is subsection (g): *Special Rule for Certain Rental Use.* This is a fascinating exception. As long as you do not claim any operating-type rental expenses, a small amount of rental income — called a "de minimis amount" — is officially overlooked on your Form 1040 tax return.

The subsection (g) of 280A reads in full as follows:

Notwithstanding any other provision of this section or section 183 [relating to not-for-profit activities], *if a dwelling unit is used during the taxable year as a residence and such dwelling unit is actually rented for less than 15 days during the taxable year, then—*

(1) no deduction otherwise allowable because of the rental use of such dwelling unit shall be allowed, and

(2) the income derived from such use for the taxable year shall not be included in the gross income of such taxpayer under section 61 [relating to gross income defined]. [Emphasis added.]

The emphasized phrase "actually rented" refers to fair rental days only. If you rent your vacation/second home at competitive market rates for less than 15 days, you *do not* have to include the rental receipts on your Form 1040 tax return. Subsection (g)(2) is very specific — and very clear — on this point.

What happens if you rent to family, friends, and neighbors at below fair market rates?

This is the fascinating part.

It is unlikely that you would rent to strangers at below fair market rates. But if you rented to friends and neighbors at rates that approximately offset your operating expenses (other than property taxes and mortgage interest), would there be any need to report your rental receipts?

The answer is "No." You did not actually rent at fair market rates.

Days rented at below market rates do not count as fair rental days. They count as personal use days. For all personal use days, your only allowable deductions are property taxes and mortgage interest. Thus, if your below market rental receipts were deliberately set to offset your nontax, noninterest expenses (such as insurance, repairs, supplies, cleaning, utilities, association dues, etc.), the whole affair would be a *tax wash*. Therefore, no tax reporting of the rental receipts would be required.

Determining Fair Rental Days

If you want to claim all applicable/allocable operating expenses and depreciation deductions on your vacation home, you must establish and keep track of your fair rental days. This means that you must keep a *fair rental diary*. In this diary, you list the name and permanent home address of each tenant. You also show the rental period and the amount of rent that he/she/they paid. You do this on the premise that you are renting — or have it available for rent — to more than one market rate tenant during the year.

"How does one determine a fair rental day?" you ask.

One way to do this is to canvass the general area where your vacation home is located, and make direct inquiry to those property owners who are also renting out their homes to the general public. Ask what rates they charge. Ask what the rate fluctuations are between peak-season and off-season. Ask what advertising sources produce the best tenants.

Or, you can look through the "For Rent" ads in local newspapers and on public bulletin boards. Then go visit the offered property yourself and make comparisons with your property. Prepare written notes on the comparable rentals, in case you need to prove to some skeptical IRS agent that you are indeed charging a fair rental rate.

Probably a better way to document fair rental rates is to visit one or more real estate rental agencies in the vicinity of your vacation property. Ask for copies of whatever listings they have on properties currently rented or available for rent. Pay an appraisal fee, and have at least one rental agency prepare a fair rental statement for you. Make sure the statement includes a description of your property, and the number of days out of 365 days per year that you intend to offer it for rent. Have the appraisal statement specify the peak rental months and the low rental months. In popular vacation areas, the peak rental rates may be as much as five times the off-peak (low demand) months.

If you want the extra tax benefits of deducting operating expenses and depreciation, you are expected to put forth the necessary effort to establish and keep track of your fair rental days.

Fair Rental Expense Allocations

Subsection (e) of 280A: *Expenses Attributable to* [Fair] *Rental*, constitutes the core essence of the vacation home rental rules. But, we want to warn you: Subsection (e)(1) is fuzzy, ambiguous, wordy, and . . . misleading. It leaves you open to all kinds of interpretation abuses by the IRS.

Here's what subsection (e) of 280A tries to say. It tries to say that *all expenses* — those listed in Figure 4.3 plus the depreciation exemplified in Figure 2.4 — must be apportioned by the ratio of the ' fair rental days to the total use days (personal plus rental) for the year. Vacant days in a 365-day year do not count.

In other words, the Applicable Expense Ratio (AER) that applies to each expense total for the year is:

$$\text{AER} = \frac{\text{Number of Fair Rental Days}}{\substack{\text{Total Use Days (fair rental, plus personal use,}\\ \text{plus below-market rentals)}}}$$

Suppose that you, your family, and below-market others used the vacation home for 31 days out of the year. Your fair rental diary shows that you actually rented it for 185 days. What is your tax qualified AER (Applicable Expense Ratio)?

It is—

$$\frac{185}{185+31} = \frac{185}{216} = 0.8564$$

or 85.64%

Thus, you would multiply all Figure 4.3 expenses by this AER, as well as all Figure 2.4 depreciation. For the example days cited, your unallowed rental expenses would be about 15% of your annual totals.

If you reduced your personal use days from 31 to 20, say, for the same fair rental days, your AER would increase to 90%. Suppose you reduced your personal use days to 16. That would be less than 10% of your fair rental days (10% x 185 days = 18.5

days). In this case, the AER factor would not apply. You get 100% of your applicable expenses. The reason is you used the property less than "the greater of" 14 days or 10% of the fair rental days. When the fair rental days exceed 140, the 10% portion of the trigger rule is more tax beneficial (10% of 140 is 14 days).

Subsection (e) Actual Wording

We've tried above to present in layman language the essence of subsection (e) of 280A: Expenses attributable to rental (at fair market rates). We may have been successful. Yet we may not have been.

If you think the above is ambiguous to any degree, compare our presentation with the actual tax law wording. Subsection (e) reads essentially in full as follows:

> *(e)* *Expenses Attributable to Rental.*
> *(1)* *In general. In any case where a taxpayer who is an individual . . . uses a dwelling unit for personal purposes on any day during the taxable year (whether or not he is treated under this section as using such unit as a residence), the amount deductible under this chapter with respect to expenses attributable to the rental of the unit (or portion thereof) for the taxable year shall not exceed an amount which bears the same relationship to such expenses as the number of days during each year that the unit (or portion thereof) is rented at a fair rental bears to the total number of days during such year that the unit (or portion thereof) is used.*
> *(2)* *Exception for deductions otherwise allow-able. This subsection shall not apply with respect to deductions which would be allowable under this chapter for the taxable year whether or not such unit (or portion thereof) was rented.*

The key point embedded in this statutory language is the number of days (personal plus rental) that the vacation home is **used** during each tax accountable year. The language is silent on what happens to the nonuse or vacant days. You still have expenses and depreciation for those days. Now what?

The IRS says: "That's tough." You get no rental-type deductions whatsoever for nonuse days. Even if the property is offered, available, and totally ready for rent, and there are no takers, you get no deduction. This is the stringency of the vacation home rental rules.

What about property taxes, mortgage interest, and casualty losses during those nonuse/vacant days? [Subsection (e)(2) above is subsection (b) revisited.]

The IRS says that you may claim the prorata nonuse portions as itemized (personal) deductions on Schedule A (Form 1040), if you otherwise qualify. But you cannot claim them on Schedule E (Form 1040) as vacant rental property.

Now for "Catch-22"

Suppose that your properly allocable vacation rental expenses exceed your gross fair rental income for the year. You established your AER correctly; you have your fair rental days well documented; you cut your operating expenses to the bare bones; you used very conservative depreciation schedules. Still your total attributable expenses exceed your total fair rental income. Do you have a tax recognized passive activity loss?

Again the IRS says: "Tough luck. No recognized loss."

The IRS's rationale is that you rented a vacation home; there was no profit motive when you bought it. The not-for-profit rules (Section 183) apply. The only concession you get is that your unallowed attributable losses can be carried over to a subsequent fair rental tax year. The supposition is that you may want to increase your rents the following year.

Which unallowed attributable losses are carried over? There's a 3-step priority procedure to follow. We portray this priority sequence in Figure 6.2.

Priority 1 uses property taxes and mortgage interest to reduce your rental income (designated as *Class I* expenses). Priority 2 uses your operating expenses (insurance, repairs, utilities, etc.) to reduce your rental income (designated as *Class II* expenses). And Priority 3 is your scheduled depreciation (designated as *Class III* expenses). At whatever point in this reduction hierarchy your net income reduces to zero, your remaining unusable deductions are disallowed . . . for that year. You then have the task of keeping track of your attributable unallowed losses for possibly using them in subsequent years.

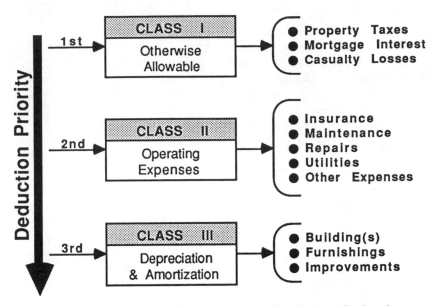

Fig. 6.2 - Expense Classifications for Prioritizing Deductions

Qualified Rental Periods

If all of the above is too much for you, and you are serious about wanting to rent your vacation/second home for profit, there is a very practical way out. List your property with an established real estate rental agency. Sign a rental contract for no less than 12 consecutive months. Have the rental agency do all the advertising, collect all rents, pay all operating expenses, and report to you periodically the net cash proceeds, if any. Your rental contract should specify that any cash shortage is made up by you (which **is** tax deductible). Taxwise, this arrangement is treated as a *qualified rental period*.

Let us explain.

If you rent your vacation home under conditions called a "qualified rental period," you need not establish fair rental days. Nor do personal use days become a tax-qualifying concern. You may use the property all you want before or after the qualified rental period . . . but not during it.

As per subsection 280A(d)(4)(B), the term qualifying rental period means—

A consecutive period of—
(i) 12 or more months which begins or ends in [the] *taxable year, or*
(ii) less than 12 months which begins in such taxable year and at the end of which such dwelling unit is sold or exchanged, and—
for which such unit is rented **or is held for rental***, at a fair rental.* [Emphasis added.]

A consecutive 12-month period "held for rental" would be your entering into an enforceable rental-listing contract with an established real estate firm. By so doing, the tax law rationale is that you have knowingly converted your vacation home into bona fide rental property seeking a profit. Thereupon, the vacation home (attributable expense) rental rules would not apply.

As with any rental-listing contract, there will be bona fide periods of nonrental. There will be off-season vacancies, and short-term vacancies between old tenants moving out and new tenants moving in. During these nonrental periods, should you visit the property to do cleaning, painting, repairs, and maintenance, such visits would not count as personal use.

Renting Rooms in Your Home

Suppose you have a 3-bedroom house, each room with its own adjoining bath, which you use as your primary residence. It is not a vacation home nor a second home. Your children are grown (or you are divorced or widowed), so you decide to rent out two of the bedrooms. You need the extra income. Are you restricted by the vacation house rental rules?

Yes, but to a lesser degree of stringency. Not being a vacation/second home, establishing fair rental days would not be a dominating concern. As your regular home, chances are it would be in a metropolitan area or accessible to such area. As such, you'd be renting it on a 6-month, 12-month, or longer consecutive period. Thus, your rental intent would be the same as a "qualified rental period" above. Instead of listing your rooms with a rental agency, you'd be the on-site rental manager yourself.

Your applicable Schedule E expense allocations take on a different twist from that of a vacation home rental. You have to allocate all of your annual property expenses in direct proportion to the fraction of the home that is being rented, and the fraction in which you reside. It is as though you owned *two* properties: a rental property and a residence property. You do the fractionation by measuring the square footage of each property.

When renting rooms in your home, the separately occupied spaces (such as bedrooms, baths, hallways, etc.) can be separately measured. But what about the commonly shared areas: kitchen, living room, family room, den, etc? You still measure the square footage, but you allocate between rental and nonrental in proportion to the number of persons who use those common areas. The end result is that you compile a composite rental-use fraction (RUF) which you apply across the board to all of your Schedule E-type expenses.

Subsection (c)(3) of 280A appears to support this home rental use concept. Specifically, subsection (c)(3) says—

> *(c)* **Exceptions for Certain Business or Rental Use; Limitation on Deductions for Such Use.**
> *(3) Rental use. Subsection (a) shall not apply to any item which is attributable to the rental of the dwelling unit or portion thereof (determined after the application of subsection (e)).*

The phrase "or portion thereof" expressly permits renting of rooms and establishing the percentage of total living space applicable to such rental use.

The limitation on deductions when renting rooms in your home is set forth in subsection (c)(5). In essence, your total deductions are prioritized into the same three Figure 6.2 classes (I, II, and III) as under the vacation home rules. Then, as you go down the deduction classes, their allowability ceases the moment they equal or exceed your gross rental income for the year.

However, if the designated rental/business portion of your primary residence is not used for personal purposes, and you at all times charge fair rental values, then any net negative rental income is allowed. You, in effect, have converted a portion of your home into a profit-seeking venture. This would be especially true if you ran a bed and breakfast type inn, or used a portion of your home for providing day care services.

7

SHARED EQUITY RENTALS

Subsection 280A(d)(3)(B)(i) Of The Tax Code Blesses The Rental Arrangement Known As: "Shared Equity Financing Agreement" (SEFA). This Is Tenants-In-Common Ownership Between Two Or More Separate Parties. One, The Owner-Tenant, Occupies The Property As A Principal Residence And Pays Rent To The Owner-Nonoccupant. The Owner-Tenant Gets Certain Schedule A Tax Benefits, Whereas The Owner-Nonoccupant Gets Prorata Schedule E Benefits. A Target Date For Property Sale Is Set, At Which Time The Equity Buildup Is Split Pursuant To The SEFA Terms.

A variant form of rental property co-ownership is "shared equity." This is an arrangement whereby two or more parties, who are not husband and wife, get together to purchase a dwelling unit with the expectation of selling it and sharing in the profits. It is this profit expectation that removes the property from the vacation home rules.

The term "equity" means value minus debt. In the case of a dwelling unit, equity is market value minus mortgage debt. The buildup of equity or capital — in which the sharing takes place — derives from the initial capital contributed, the capital improvements made, and by market appreciation over time.

A shared equity *rental* is a dwelling unit whereby one of the parties becomes the owner-occupant, and the other party becomes the owner-investor. The owner-investor rents his portion of the unit to the owner-occupant. The amount of rent charged must be the fair rental rate at the time the property is acquired.

The rental arrangement requires that there be at least two different parties with ownership interests. A husband and wife, by the way, constitute one ownership interest. There can be three, four, or more ownership interests. However, experience has shown that when there are more than three ownership interests (including spouses), the tax accounting details of the arrangement become complex and unwieldy. Frictions and misunderstandings invariably arise. When they do, the month-to-month accounting and record keeping become slipshod and unreliable.

For best results, equity sharing arrangements should last no more than three to five years. This is sufficient time for the property, if well maintained, to increase in value. Each ownership interest then can take his/her/their share of the profits and go separately onto other dwelling units or to investment activities.

In this chapter, we want to discuss the tax law pertinent to shared equity arrangements, the tax accounting required, and the opportunity benefits to the various owners. First, let's address the owner-occupant: the rental tenant.

Owner-Occupant: Tenant

It is a fact of life that most tenants of rental real estate would someday like to own their own home. This is particularly true for young adults, just-marrieds, divorced persons, and single parents. For most individuals, owning a home is the most important single investment in their entire life. It requires, initially, a large amount of capital relative to one's savings or sources of income. Therefore, if someone else comes along who is willing to share in the capital (money) requirement, there is opportunity for each of the sharing parties to benefit.

The principal benefit to the owner-occupant is the opportunity to acquire at least a partial ownership interest in a dwelling unit, that he might not otherwise be able to acquire. This is especially attractive to first-time home buyers. The fact that the most successful equity sharing arrangements last no more than three to five years gives the owner-occupant time to build up his own savings and gain some equity profit, too. When the shared equity unit is sold, the owner-occupant usually has amassed enough cash to subsequently buy a home on his own. In the meantime, he is part-tenant and part-owner in a "starter home."

The success of a shared equity rental arrangement depends on each party understanding and fulfilling his percent-equity role. If there is a 50/50 equity role, for example, the owner-occupant (tenant) must stick to his 50% throughout the ownership period. Likewise, the owner-investor (landlord) must stick to his 50% role throughout the ownership period. These roles tend to be in opposition to each other, and if maintained so, constitute the very legitimacy of shared equity rental for tax purposes. To help you visualize these contrasting roles, we present Figure 7.1.

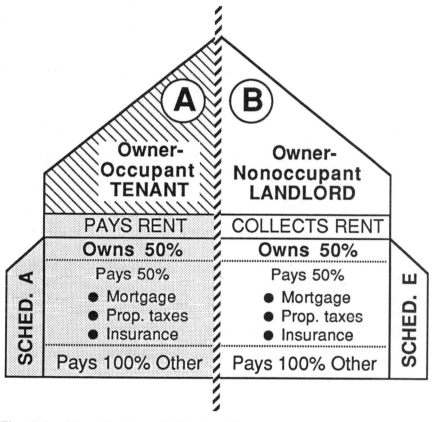

Fig. 7.1 - Visualization of "Equity Sharing" in a Residential Rental

Although we show a 50/50 arrangement in Figure 7.1, it could be 35/65 or 65/35, or some other percentage split. The arrangement could start with one percentage split and end with a different percentage split. For example, the owner-occupant (tenant) could start with a 35% ownership interest. Depending on terms acceptable to the owner-investor (landlord), the tenant could end up with 50% or higher ownership interest. In other words, there is — or could be — opportunity for the owner-occupant to enhance his ownership interest throughout the rental period . . . or vice versa.

Ownership: Tenants-in-Common

In the ordinary sense, a "tenant" is a person who pays rent to occupy or use land and its structural appurtenances (buildings, etc.). In a more formal sense, a tenant may also be a person who possesses land (and its appurtenances) by any form of legal title. In a shared equity situation, both tenants share a common title to the property. The most accepted legal form in this regard is TENANTS IN COMMON.

When property is held in tenancy in common, each tenant possesses an undivided interest in that property. It is "undivided" in the sense that, being a dwelling unit, it cannot be literally cut or divided into each owner's specific ownership share. By glancing back at Figure 7.1, you can readily see that it is impractical — and it would destroy the property's value — to cut it down the middle for the 50/50 split. Hence, tenancy in common is the proper legal form of ownership, regardless of the specific percentage of ownership of each co-owner. This form preserves the individual right of each tenant in common to transfer his undivided interest to someone else during his lifetime, or upon his death.

As we introduced to you back in Chapter 1, the ownership of real estate is evidenced by a legal instrument called a *title deed*. When the property is purchased in a market-valued transaction, the most common deed form is a Grant Deed. The contents of such a deed were outlined in Figure 1.1. We suggest that you take a moment now to review that figure. It is located on page 1-4. While at it, glance at the accompanying text, and review the procedure for official recordation of title to property.

The key legal feature of tenants in common is that each co-owner's fractional interest in the property can be precisely specified, if so desired. For example, if there were three co-owners: A, B, and C, the fractional interest of each could be specified as—

Owner A   —   29.64%
Owner B   —   46.83%

Owner C   —   <u>23.53%</u>
Total   —   100.00%

For equity sharing situations, Owner A could be the occupying tenant, and Owners B and C could be the investing landlords. By such specificity in the title, and its recordation in official records, the ownership percentages are cast in concrete. Should, for whatever reason, the ownership percentages change, a new title deed would be required.

The really nice feature about tenants in common is that each owner's individual property rights can be preserved without actually specifying the precise percentages. The individual percentage can be left to another written instrument which is "incorporated by reference" in the title deed. This latter phrase is common legal wording for accessing supplemental documents.

For example, a shared equity tenants-in-common title might read as—

For valuable consideration . . . etc.

XYZ, seller—
HEREBY GRANTS TO—

Party A: John and Mary Jones, husband and wife,
AND TO—
Party B: Henry and Jean Adams, husband and wife,
where Parties A and B are TENANTS IN COMMON, of which each party's percentage ownership is stated in that SHARED EQUITY FINANCING AGREEMENT, dated _____,
which is incorporated herein by reference,

that certain parcel of land, together with its building and appurtenances, described as follows, to wit:

Because of the ownership fine points of tenancy in common, and the ever-present possibility of legal controversies arising, we recommend shared equity arrangement only between family members and close blood relatives. We do not recommend such arrangements with strangers, distant relatives, or nonblood participants. In nonblood-tenant situations, too many legal problems can arise in the event of ownership disputes.

Rental to Family Members

In Chapter 6 (Vacation Home Rentals), there was much ado about residential property being "rented" to family members. The tax law on point was Section 280A of which subsection (a) disallowed — generally — all landlord-type expenses therewith. Now we want to tell you about a special exception.

This exception is a shared equity rental arrangement expressly identified in subsection 280A(**d**)(**3**). The official heading to this subsection reads: *Rental to family members, etc., for use as a principal residence.*

Subsection 280A(d)(3)(**A**) — the "in general" part — reads in full as follows:

> *A taxpayer shall not be treated as using a dwelling unit for personal purposes by reason of a rental arrangement for any period if for such period such dwelling unit is rented, at a fair rental, to any person for use as such person's principal residence.*

In the context of Section 280A, the term "taxpayer" is the owner of a residential-type real estate which is not his primary home. This is the owner-investor that we described above. If the property is rented at fair value to someone else who uses the property as his principal residence, the vacation/second home rules do not apply. This "someone else" is the owner-occupant that we also described above.

As you may have noted in the statutory wording of subsection (d)(3)(A), the tax blessing of shared equity rental is not limited to family members. The specific tax law phrase used is: *any person.* Tax law has to be written this way, to avoid its criticism for taxpayer favoritism. Interestingly, however, the official heading to (d)(3) does use the phrase "family member." This would imply that Congress preferred that shared equity rentals be primarily between family members.

To lend support to this Congressional preference, we look to the immediately preceding tax code subsection, namely: (d)(2)(A). Its official heading is: Personal use of unit. The clause pertinent to our discussion is—

> *. . . or by any member of the family (as defined in section 267(c)(4)) of the taxpayer . . .*

Section 267(c)(4) defines a family member as:

The family of an individual shall include only his brothers and sisters (whether by the whole or half blood), spouse, ancestors, and lineal descendants.

Must Own "Appurtenant Land"

Subsection 280A(d)(3)(**D**) attaches another condition to the tax blessing of shared equity rentals. That condition is, each equity owner must possess a *qualified ownership interest* in the dwelling unit **and** in its appurtenant land.

On this point, the express statutory wording is—

The term "qualified ownership interest" means an undivided interest for more than 50 years in the entire dwelling unit and appurtenant land being acquired in the transaction to which the shared equity . . . relates.

There are a lot of real estate legalities in this "appurtenant land" requirement. In the first place, it rules out all forms of dwelling units which are not structurally fixed to land. Living units such as boats, trailers, campers, motor homes, mobile homes, and the like are precluded. This preclusion prevails even if the structures are comparable in size and accommodations to fixed structures on land.

Secondly, the "more than 50 years" clause requires that the land be owned in *fee simple*. This is a legal term meaning absolute ownership with unrestricted rights of disposition. This rules out 99-year-type leases of land rent contracts, still practiced in some realty areas of the U.S. The perpetual renting of land is a carryover from the ancient days of feudalism. In those days, fee simple meant that land could only be inherited by lineal descendants of the original landlord. Thus, if the dwelling unit land cannot be acquired in fee simple, equity sharing rental arrangements are disqualified for tax purposes.

And, thirdly, we take note of the statutory phrase "undivided interest" in subsection (d)(3)(D). This reverts back to the tenants-in-common ownership form that we described earlier. In other words, it is the land — principally — that must be acquired in tenants-in-common form. Therefore, a qualified dwelling unit consists of land, a fixed building, and other structural appurtenances. This seems to rule out equity sharing arrangements involving the accompanying rental of furniture, fixtures, furnishings, and movable appliances. Presumably, the owner-occupant is required to buy these items himself.

Written Agreement Required

Another tax qualification for equity sharing is that the arrangement be in writing. The tax code itself does not expressly say this. It requires that a formal document be prepared which is designated as a Shared Equity Financing Agreement: SEFA. Any arrangement involving a financial agreement with respect to real estate must be in writing. Most all states in the U.S. require this. So, too, does the IRS. Oral agreements simply will not stand up two, three, or more years after the property acquisition.

On this point, subsection 280A(d)(3)(B)(i) specifically says—

Subparagraph (A) [regarding use as a personal residence] *shall apply to a rental to a person who has an interest in the dwelling unit **only** if such rental is pursuant to a shared equity financing agreement.* [Emphasis added.]

Subsection (d)(3(C) goes on to define what is meant by a SEFA. The tax code says—

The term "shared equity financing agreement" means an agreement under which—
(i) 2 or more persons acquire qualified ownership interests in a dwelling unit, and
(ii) the person (or persons) holding 1 or more of such interests—
  (I) is entitled to occupy the dwelling unit for use as a personal residence, and
  (II) is required to pay rent to 1 or more other persons holding qualified ownership interests in the dwelling unit.
[The] *fair rental shall be determined as of the time the agreement is entered into and by taking into account the occupant's qualified ownership interest.*

Here, again, the statutory language does not specifically say that the SEFA shall be in writing. It is certainly well implied. There is no other acceptable way. Obviously, there has to be some sort of reference document (in the event of dispute later) in which the separate ownership interests are set forth, the terms of sharing are disclosed, and the amount of rent to be paid is agreed upon. Just what form the document needs to be is up to the participants and local custom regarding rental realty matters.

Basic Contents of SEFA

As a reminder, the acronym SEFA stands for: Shared Equity Financing Agreement. To be tax acceptable, each SEFA document must include certain basic features. Foremost is identification of the parties, the residential property acquired (or to be acquired), and signatures of the parties in the presence of a notary public. Notarized signatures on a SEFA are important for alleviating problems regarding the effective date of the arrangement and its equity terms. Whether an attorney draws up the SEFA or not is up to the parties themselves. Either way, once notarized it becomes a legal instrument if need be.

Preferably, a SEFA should be no longer than *two* typewritten or computer-printed standard stationery pages. Above all, it should be explicit about the tax and financial obligations of each party: the occupant(s) and nonoccupant(s). It should describe the purchase arrangement (down payment, loan points, mortgage payments), the fair rent to be paid, and how it shall be determined. The tax-reporting obligations of each party while holding the property, and at time of sale, should be spelled out. So, too, should the records required for equity-sharing distributions at time of sale. A target date for the sale, such as "no less than 3 years; no more than 5 years" should be stated. A target date for sale provides tax conviction of the profit motives involved.

Basically, every (tax) qualified SEFA should contain eight blocks of information, as outlined in Figure 7.2. The details for each information block will vary, of course, depending on the parties and their relationship, the realty practices in the area of the property shared, the financial capabilities of the parties, and on the tax benefits accruing to each party separately. If the percentage of ownership should change between time of purchase and time of sale, the records required for establishing the change should be set forth. We should caution you, though, that unless each SEFA party is astute at capital accounting, and the tracing/substantiation rules therewith, it is best to stick with fixed equity percentages from start to finish.

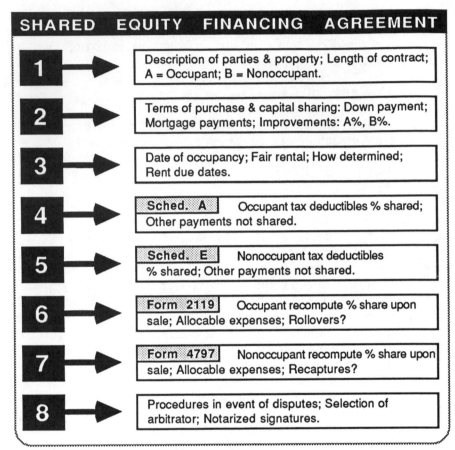

Fig. 7.2 - Information Required in a Tax Qualified SEFA

Many equity sharers do not realize that their tax benefits differ substantially from each other. For example, at time of purchase, the down payment provides no tax benefits to either party. It's a starting point for each party's capital accounting. On the other hand, the loan fee (points) associated with the mortgage contract is deductible by the owner-occupant. It is not deductible to the nonoccupant owner. Property taxes and mortgage interest are deductible by both parties, split as stated in their SEFA. Insurance, repairs, utilities are not deductible by the occupant; they are deductible by the nonoccupant to the extent actually paid. Depreciation is deductible by the nonoccupant, but not by the occupant. At time of sale, the occupant reports his share of the deal on Form 2119 (Sale of Your Home), whereas the nonoccupant reports on Form 4797 (Sales of Business Property).

A Parent-Child Example

Let's take a situation where Henry and Jean Adams (fictitious names, of course) are the parents of daughter Mary. Mary recently married John Jones. Both John and Mary have jobs, but they do not have enough money to buy their first home on their own. So the parents agree to a SEFA arrangement with their daughter and son-in-law.

John and Mary find the home that they want, but they can't afford the 20% down payment. They can afford to split the mortgage payments equitably. They badly want to be home owners.

Suppose the house that John and Mary want costs $210,000 *plus* $5,000 in closing costs (which include a $3,000 loan fee). Thus, the acquisition cost becomes $215,000. The 20% down payment required is $43,000. The parents pay $40,000 and the children pay $3,000 . . . to cover the loan fee. The mortgage is $172,000 payable over 30 years at a fixed rate of interest. Since the mortgage company will make all parties (Henry and Jean, the parents, and John and Mary, the children) co-liable whether in the SEFA or not, John and Mary recognize that they have to make 50% of the mortgage payments. All parties agree to sell the property in five years' time, with a fixed equity share of each throughout. What are the respective ownership percentages of the parents and of John and Mary?

The answer—

	Total	Parents	John & Mary
Down Payment	43,000	40,000	3,000
Mortgage Principal	172,000	86,000	86,000
	215,000	126,000	89,000
Acquisition Ownership	100%	58.60%	41.40%

The parties dislike the "odd percentages" that derive from the purchase arrangement. They want a more clean-cut 60/40 split: 60% parents, 40% children. It'll be easier this way, for five years of tax accounting. The property needs some immediate capital improvements costing $10,000. How much do the parents pay, and how much do the children pay, to bring their equity sharing to a fixed 60/40?

At this point,the total capital investment in the house becomes $225,000 ($215,000 upon acquisition plus $10,000 improvements). The parents' 60% of this amount becomes $135,000; the children's 40% becomes $90,000. Thus, the $10,000 immediate improvements would be paid as follows:

	Total	Parents	John & Mary
Acquisition	215,000	126,000	89,000
Improvements	10,000	9,000	1,000
	225,000	135,000	90,000
Ownership fixed at:		60%	40%

"Must Make" Separate Payments

Too often, SEFA arrangements fall apart because of the "horsetrading" that goes on between the parties. Usually, the occupants are young persons whose wants often outstrip their pocketbooks. The nonoccupants are usually older persons who have managed to save a little, over the years. From time to time, the occupants will be cash short and try to prevail upon the nonoccupants for some sort of trade or barter for certain payments due. This happens particularly where parents and children are SEFA involved.

To keep matters tax clean, each party must make his/her/their own separate payments. For example, suppose the agreement is 50/50 on the monthly mortgage payments. When due, each mortgage payment is made with *two separate* checks. Check A for 50% is paid by the parents; check B for 50% is paid by the children. The mortgage company doesn't care how many checks come in, as long as the proper total amount is paid. The same applies to other payments, such as property taxes, hazard insurance, necessary repairs, and so on.

If the parents want to make informal loans or gifts to their children for certain payments, that's fine. Just make sure that the loaned or gifted amount is first deposited in the children's account, from which they write their own checks. A nonoccupant should make no payments on behalf of the occupant, or vice versa. At all times when co-payments are required, co-payments should be made. Despite all the convenience and simplicity of "electronic banking" these days, hand-written checks which are cancelled are still the best tax evidence of payments made.

The real tax test of a SEFA arrangement is the payment of monthly rent by the owner-occupant to nonoccupant owner. In all cases, the fair market rate must be paid . . . *taking into consideration the occupant's ownership interest.* Where parents and children are involved, a more convincing fair rental would be a certified statement by a professional real estate appraiser. The monthly rate should be fixed on or prior to the first day of occupancy by the owner-occupant.

In the parents and John and Mary illustration above, suppose the fair market rent were documented as $1,500 per month. How much would John and Mary actually have to pay to their parents?

Answer: $900 per month. This is 60% x $1,500 which is $900. After all, John and Mary are only renting 60% of the home; they own the other 40% themselves. Therefore, there is no need for them to pay the full 100% fair rent to their parents. This same principle applies whether the occupants are family related or not.

Owner Differences: Schedules A & E

Let's continue with the parents and John and Mary SEFA example above. The parents agree to pay 60% of the property taxes, hazard insurance, and necessary repairs. They may pay voluntarily other costs such as association dues, painting and fixup, selected gardening, pool service, and other operating-type costs which do not alter their ownership percentage of 60%.

John and Mary agree to pay 40% of the property taxes, hazard insurance, and necessary repairs. They also agree to pay — as they should — 100% of all consumption-type expenses, such as ordinary cleaning and maintenance, all utilities, regular gardening, trash removal, and the like.

Both parties agree to each make 1/2 of the mortgage payments. One reason for this is because all parties are equally co-liable. The tax reason for equal mortgage payments is that it keeps the 60/40 ownership split fixed throughout the SEFA period. The part of the mortgage payment that goes to principal is part of each party's capital basis in the property. The parties agree that if any further capital improvements are to be made, the costs will be split 60/40.

Assume that the interest payments on the mortgage average $1,200 per month. This figure, of course, will vary, but assume that this is the five-year average. Further assume that property taxes average $2,400 per year, hazard insurance averages $800 per year, and all other shared expenses average $500 per year. What information would go on the parents' and on the children's respective tax returns?

Attached to John and Mary's Form 1040, there would be **Schedule A**: Itemized (Personal) Deductions. They would enter on Schedule A 40% of the property taxes and 50% of the mortgage interest. They would also enter 100% of the loan fee as "deductible points" which they paid. That's all. They'd get nothing for insurance, repairs, gardening, utilities, etc. They would, however, be allowed other personal deductions which are non-SEFA.

Attached to the parents' Form 1040, there would be **Schedule E**: Supplemental Income or Loss. They would enter on Schedule E 60% of the property taxes, 50% of the mortgage interest, 60% of the hazard insurance, 60% of necessary repairs, and 100% of the operating expenses actually paid. Moreover, they would have to set up a Depreciation Schedule (Form 4562) showing:

Total basis in property	$225,000
Assessor's land portion	65,000
Dwelling unit portion	160,000
60% rental portion	96,000
27.5-year straight-line	3,490/year

Still further, they would have to enter the rental income on Schedule E. If the total deductions produced a net loss, they would have to prepare Form 8582: Passive Activity Loss Limitations.

To produce any net tax benefit to John and Mary, their total deductions on Schedule A must exceed the standard nonitemized deductions (of around $7,000 for a joint return; changes each year). To produce any net tax benefits to the parents, their total deductions on Schedule E must exceed the rental income (of about $10,800). There is no requirement that the tax benefits to each party match their 60/40 SEFA split. Said split is mandatory only at time of sale of the property.

8

FARMLAND RENTALS

In Many Rural Areas, Sharecropping Is A Way of Life. A Landowner Leases (Rents) His Land To A Tenant Farmer Who Supplies The Machinery And Labor To Work The Land And Harvest The Crops (And/Or Livestock). For This, The Tenant Gets (Typically) 65% Of The Harvest. The Owner Gets 35%. The Landowner Reports His Noncash Rents On Form 4835: FARM RENTAL INCOME AND EXPENSES. Most Land-Servicing And Maintenance Expenses Are Allowed, Including As Many As 15 Different Depreciation Schedules. Any Net Loss Is Subject To The Same Limitation Rules Of Other Rental Real Estate.

A variant of the equity-sharing features in Chapter 7 is the sharecropping of farmland. In a sharecropping arrangement, the owner of the land is often an absentee. He does not work his land. He engages a tenant who provides all of the machinery and labor for planting and harvesting crops and/or the stocking and raising of livestock. The tenant pays no rent until the crops and livestock are sold. When so sold, pledged, or subsidized, the tenant and landowner share in the proceeds in accordance with their written sharing agreement.

Farmland in and of itself is not of great value. Its value accrues only if someone is willing to put money into it to make it produce. We are talking about land which is useful only for root crops, surface crops, vines, trees, poultry, livestock, and cattle. We are not talking about land which has known mineral resources, or that which is just outside city limits where future development is likely. We are talking about plain old country-type farmland.

These days, it is unlikely that an individual investor would go into the countryside and buy up acres of land just to sharecrop it out. He might purchase land for residential or commercial property in suburban areas, but not for farmland.

Owning farmland as an *individual* is more often an inherited matter. The land — be it large or small in acreage — is usually handed down from generation to generation. If it is not directly inherited, the desire for ownership stems from strong ancestral ties to a particular land area. Somewhere along the line, there is a family heritage to be maintained. However acquired, few owners of such land intend to farm it themselves. So they sharecrop it out.

When you sharecrop farmland, it takes on the same tax character as any other form of rental real estate. In this chapter, therefore, we want to cover the distinguishing features involved, and the tax forms and tax benefits therewith. As you will soon see below, there **are** significant tax benefits in owning farmland. Even if you do not own any such land yourself, the tax benefits may be of interest to you in partnership with other members of your farm-connected family.

Rent in Noncash Form

With respect to rental income, there is one particular feature which distinguishes farm rentals from other real estate. There is no fixed certain monthly rate. There are months in which no income is derived whatsoever. The rent, when it does come, is in noncash form: produce, grain, poultry, livestock, and other crops.

In a sharecropping rental, no income can be derived until the crops are harvested and the livestock are grown. Even then, it is a matter of getting the crops to market. Not always do farm products go directly to consumers or wholesalers. In most cases, the products are "sold" through *farmers' cooperatives*. The cooperatives store or sell the products when market conditions are right. So widespread is the practice that there are separate tax laws (Sections 1381-1388) and tax forms which address cooperative selling.

In some cases, before actual assignment to a cooperative, the tenant and landlord will split the crops and livestock among themselves. Each may have his own reason for arranging separate sales. There is no requirement that both sell simultaneously.

The moment the crops are split, and the landlord takes possession of his share, he has constructively received his rents due. The problem he may have is ascertaining fair market value at the time his share is received. Presumably, at some point in time he will receive either (a) cash money, (b) line of credit, (c) barter services, (d) equipment transfer, (e) property interests, or (f) some form of contractual rights (in "certificate" form).

The point that we are trying to get across is that the rent does not come in regular monthly checks, the way rents are received from residential or commercial buildings in an urban area. It may all come at one time; it may be deferred; or it may not come at all.

Sharecropping is subject to the whims of nature. In years of severe drought, deep freeze, rampant floods, or killer tornadoes, growing crops and livestock may be destroyed in their entirety. To prepare against total rental loss, disaster claims, insurance programs, and commodity hedges are used. These are potential relief payments; they constitute substitute rents. When such payments are indeed received, they become tax accountable farm rental income.

"Typical" Sharecropping Arrangement

There's probably no such thing as a "typical" sharecropping arrangement. This is because, in different farming communities, the terms of such an arrangement will vary, depending on the farm location and size, the type of crop and livestock to be produced, local sharecropping practices, and the capabilities and needs of the participating parties. In all cases, though, one fact is clear. The landowner has hundreds of acres of farmland which needs to be worked; the tenant-sharecropper is in need of work but has no land . . . or not enough on his own. The two parties get together to discuss their own arrangement to the degree of formality with which each is comfortable.

The canvassing of prospects for sharecropping tenants is by word of mouth, such as through family referrals, farmers' cooperatives, supply store billboards, and local advertising media. In those areas where sharecropping is a way of life, the word can get around pretty quickly that a particular landowner is looking for a reliable person to till his land.

In communities where sharecropping is a well-established practice, formal LEASE AGREEMENTS are signed. The terms of the lease require that the landowner pay for all expenses associated with conservation, irrigation, revitalizing, and servicing the land. This includes the cost of barns, silos, stables, irrigation equipment, fencing, and overall general maintenance of the farm (or ranch). The tenant pays for all labor and machinery (including custom hire) for tilling the land, tending the livestock, and harvesting the crops. For such items as seed, feed, fertilizer, and chemicals, the costs are split between the landowner and tenant in accordance with their crop-split percentages. Typically (?) the landowner gets 35%; the tenant gets 65%.

Because of the mechanization of agriculture these days, tenant farming is a full-time business. Most tenant sharecroppers own a small farm of their own, where they live. By putting most of their money into farm machinery instead of in land, they can farm and harvest great acreages of other people's land. In all tax-accounting respects, tenant sharecroppers are self-employed persons.

The sharecropping agreement provides that, at time of harvest, the crops (including grain, fruit, nuts, poultry, livestock, etc.) are physically separated and identified. The landowner-tenant separation remains intact, even if the crops are transported in the same vehicle to the market place. When the crops are consigned, pledged, or sold, separate income accounts are maintained by the marketer — be it a farm cooperative or otherwise.

The overall arrangement above is more or less that which we depict in Figure 8.1. Since this is a tax book, we are stressing the tax features of such an arrangement. Taxwise, the actual terms and formality of the agreement to share are less important than the fact that there is a written agreement. The percentage of sharing — or a clear formula for determining it — must be expressly stated.

Introduction to Form 4835

Note in Figure 8.1 that we highlight two different tax forms: one for the landowner; one for the tenant. For the landowner, **Form 4835** (Farm Rental Income and Expenses) applies. For the tenant, **Schedule F** (Farm Income and Expenses) applies. In most respects, the income and expense entries on both forms are similar (if not identical). The key difference between the two forms is the treatment of the "bottom line." On Form 4835, the net rental income is not subject to social security self-employment tax. On Schedule F, the net farm income **is** subject to the *second tax*: the self-employment social security tax. The reason for this second tax is

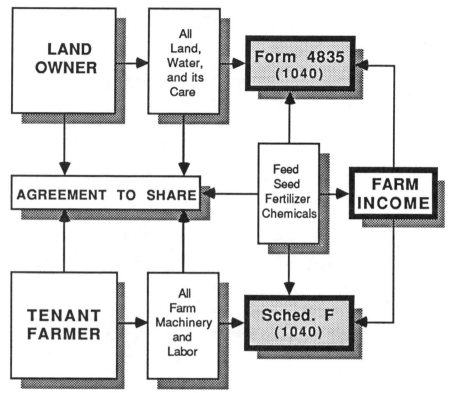

Fig. 8.1 - Tax Elements of a Sharecropping Agreement

that the tenant-sharecropper performs substantial personal services on the farm, whereas the landowner does not.

From this point on, our focus is on Form 4835 only ... and the tax pointers therewith. After all, this book is on rental real estate: not on farming. The complete official heading on Form 4835 is:

Farm Rental Income and Expenses
Crop and Livestock Shares (Not Cash) Received by Landowner (or Sub-Lessor)
Income not subject to self-employment tax
Attach to Form 1040

This heading by itself says quite a lot. The parenthesized term "not cash" means that this form is not to be used for cash rents. Cash rent would be fixed monthly rents, such as money received for

FORM 4835	FARM RENTAL INCOME & EXPENSES	YEAR

● Name of Landowner ● Type of Farm Products	Social Security No.
● Location of Farm ● Total Acres Leased	Employer I.D. No.

A Commodity Credit Corporation loans? ☐ Yes ☐ No

B Active participation in the operation? ☐ Yes ☐ No

C Preproductive period expenses? ☐ Does not apply ☐ Yes ☐ No

Part I   **Gross Farm Rental Income**

(See Fig. 8.3)

Total Rents ▶ _____

Part II   **Expenses - Farm Rental Property**

(See Fig. 8.4)

Total Expenses ▶ _____

Net Farm Rental Income or Loss ➡ _____

If a loss, you MUST answer:
☐ All investment is at risk
☐ Some investment is not at risk

If a loss, you MUST complete:
● Form 6198 ● Form 8582

Amount ▶ Deductible _____

Fig. 8.2 - General Format and Contents of Form 4835

grazing rights, recreational use, storage of other farmers' crops, and parking space for farm machinery and its servicing. The instructions tell you to report cash rents on Schedule E: not on Form 4835. This form is for crop and livestock shares only.

With the above as background, we present in Figure 8.2 a highly abbreviated arrangement of Form 4835. As you can see, it consists of headnote questions, income, expenses, and footnote instructions. Altogether there are approximately 40 line entries and approximately 10 checkboxes to be read.

Three Leadoff Questions

In Figure 8.2, we highly abbreviated the three leadoff questions designated as A, B, and C. You are expected to answer each question "Yes" or "No" and mark a checkbox accordingly. In the case of Question C, you may mark "Does not apply," if, indeed, such answer is appropriate. Each question tips you off to certain tax rules affecting farmland rentals.

The three checkbox questions are—

A. *Did you make an election in a prior year to include Commodity Credit Corporation loan proceeds as income in that year?*

B. *Did you actively participate in the operation of this farm during* [current year]*?*

C. *Did you elect, or did you previously elect, to currently deduct certain preproductive period expenses?*

Question A relates to tax code Section 77: Commodity Credit Corporation Loans. Most farming endeavors require up-front loans to get a crop in production. The CCC loans permit pledging of the crops-to-be-produced as collateral. Section 77 allows you the choice of reporting the loan proceeds as income in the year of the loan or when the crop is harvested and either sold or forfeited (to CCC). Because the loan proceeds are used for current-year farming expenses, it is often preferable to report the loan proceeds as current income.

Question B can easily be misinterpreted. The term "actively participate" means making management-type decisions and not the actual physical farming itself. One actively participates when he negotiates the rental (sharecropping) agreement, decides on which fields, fences, or roads are to be used or maintained, and arranges for the marketing of his share of the crop. Only 10% or more owners of the land can actively participate. If you answer "Yes" to Question B, you become eligible for the special $25,000 loss allowance for rental real estate activities (previously discussed).

Question C relates to Section 263A for capitalizing certain farming expenses where the preproduction period is more than two years. It does not apply to annual crop plantings, livestock, or the replacement of vines and trees destroyed by drought, freeze, pests, disease, or storms. The question is directed primarily at longstanding vineyards and orchards. Hence, unless you have a vineyard or orchard which is tenant farmed, the checkbox "Does not apply" is appropriate.

Understanding the questions above and answering them properly gives you a foretaste of the scope of tax accounting entries that go on Form 4835.

Gross Farm Rents Defined

Part I of Form 4835 carries the official heading:

Gross Farm Rental Income — Based on Production
(Include amounts converted to cash or the equivalent.)

This heading clearly targets your rental income as that which is based on production alone. Cash rents, as we mentioned above, are not reported on this form. The phrase "cash or the equivalent" means fair market value of the crops or livestock produced.

There are at least eight different types of income classed as farm rent. These all hinge on variations of the concept: *conversion* to cash or the equivalent. They are predicated upon the realization that in the business of farming, many uncontrollable events intercede to prevent direct marketing of the crops and livestock produced (or were to have been produced).

The eight types of farm rental income are presented in Figure 8.3. The listing is essentially an edited version of Part I of Form 4835. We have slightly rearranged the items and have numbered them strictly sequentially (for better instructional purposes). Some are self-explanatory; others are not so.

Line 1 in Figure 8.3 is your share of the crops and livestock marketed or exchanged under your supervision and control. You may designate an agent on the scene to do this for you. The key difference between line 1 and most other lines is that there are no "Information Returns" (of the Form 1099-series) which are sent to the IRS by payers for computer matching your entries. In other words, line 1 is that income which you establish from your own records of cash, credit, property, or services that you receive.

Lines 3 through 6 are those amounts reported to the IRS by the payers thereof. For each line, one or more of the following *information* returns is prepared:

Form 1099-A: Acquisition or Abandonment of Secured Property

Form 4835	FARM RENTAL INCOME AND EXPENSES		
Part I	**GROSS FARM RENTAL INCOME**		
1.	Income from production of livestock, produce, grains, and other crops		
2.	CCC loans reported under Question A election		
3.	CCC loans forfeited or repaid with certificates	Total	////////
		Taxable ►	
4.	Distributions from farm cooperatives	Total	////////
		Taxable ►	
5.	Agricultural program payments	Total	////////
		Taxable ►	
6.	Crop insurance proceeds and disaster payments	Total	////////
		Taxable ►	
7.	Credit for Federal tax on gasoline, diesel, and special fuels		
8.	Other income (barter, prizes, debt forgiveness, hedging transactions)		
////	**GROSS FARM RENTS** Add all of the above ━━━►		

Fig. 8.3 - Edited Listing of Income Items on Form 4835

Form 1099-G: Government Agriculture and Disaster Payments

Form 1099-MISC: Substitute Payments & Crop Insurance Proceeds

Form 1099-PATR: Patronage Distributions From Cooperatives

Form CCC-182:   Commodity Credit Corporation Payments

When received, you should total and correlate these forms with the appropriate lines on your Form 4835.

As you can see in Figure 8.3, each line — 3 through 6 — has **two** entries: one for total receipts and one for the taxable amount. Because of certain election deferments and exclusions, the taxable amount is often less than the total amount. The official instructions are not very helpful in sorting out the nontaxable portions of amounts received.

For example, the instructions regarding distributions from cooperatives (Form 1099-PATR) say—

*Show patronage dividends received in cash, and the dollar amount of qualified written notices of allocation. If you received property as patronage dividends, report the fair market value of the property as income. If you received qualified per-unit retain certificates, show the stated dollar amount of the certificate. Show amounts you received when you redeemed nonqualified written notices of allocation and nonqualified per-unit retain allocations. Because these **were not taxable when issued to you**, you must report the redemption as [rental] income.* [Emphasis added.]

It is the sum of all lines 1 through 8 in Figure 8.3 that comprises the gross rents from the farm sharing operation. As exemplified above, not all amounts in dollar equivalent are immediately taxable. This is where IRS's computer-matching problems arise, several years after Form 4835 is filed.

Nonproduction-Type Rents

Of the eight items in Figure 8.3 comprising gross income, lines 1-4 are production-type rents; lines 5-8 are nonproduction-type rents. By "production-type" we mean that income which derives directly from the market conversion of crops and livestock. This includes CCC loans and certificates, whether repaid, forfeited, or redeemed. To make this distinction clearer is why we rearranged the official listing on Form 4835, Part I.

Because of the vicissitudes of farming (over-production and natural disasters), rents are often derived even when crops or livestock are not produced, or when produced but are not marketable. This is the role of government assistance programs, disaster insurance, fuel tax credits, noncommodity bartering, and commodity hedging. These are lines 5 through 8 in Figure 8.3.

Under the auspices of the U.S. Department of Agriculture, there are at least 10 incentive programs to curtail production, conserve land, restore watersheds, prevent erosion, improve forests, and support prices. These incentives are all grouped into Section 126 of the tax code, titled: *Certain Cost-Sharing Payments*. Subsection (a) thereof states, in part, that—

Gross income does not include the excludable portion of payments received under—
[the 10 incentive programs]

Subsection (b)(1)(A) defines the "excludable portion" as that which—

is determined by the Secretary of Agriculture to be made primarily for the purpose of conserving soil and water resources, protecting or restoring the environment, improving forests, or providing a habitat for wildlife.

The government incentive payments are usually reported on Form 1099-G, though some may be reported on Form CCC-182. Although you show on Form 4835, Part I, the total amount(s) received, you determine and subtract the exclusion portion yourself, before entering the taxable portion(s) in the rental income column.

When crops and livestock are destroyed by natural causes (drought, freeze, flood, or wind), insurance proceeds and disaster payments may be received. Although all such receipts are treated as rents (there are no exclusions), the landowner may elect to defer reporting such proceeds until the following year. Code Section 451(d) permits this, especially where one is unable to replant his crops or replace his livestock immediately. A checkbox appears on Form 4835 for making this election.

The term "farm rents" also includes any allowable credits or refunds of the federal tax on gasoline, diesel, and other special fuels used in farming and other off-highway purposes. The credit or refund is claimed on Form 4136: Credit for Federal Tax on Fuels. To get the credit, the fuel must be bought at a price that includes the tax. If the cost of the fuel *and its tax* is included as an expense item in Part II of Form 4835, then the credit or refund becomes taxable income the following year. This is line 7 in Figure 8.3.

Other nonproduction-type income (line 8) derives from those barter arrangements not involving crops or livestock, prizes and awards, debt forgiveness, and profits from commodity-price hedging transactions. The purchase, sale, and expiration of commodity futures contracts, if solely for the purpose of protecting you from wild price changes, are a form of business insurance. Any profits therefrom are income; any losses are an expense.

Many Expenses Allowed

For a landowner in a farming operation, there is a great variety of expenses which, if directly related to the production of crops and livestock, are deductible in the year paid or incurred. There are just three exceptions, namely:

1. Personal and family living expenses.
2. Preproductive period costs that are required to be capitalized.
3. Limited expenses for soil and water conservation.

In other respects, there are some 25 categories of farm rental expenses which are fully recognized for tax purposes. Towards this end, we present in Figure 8.4 a complete listing of all those expense categories found in Part II of Form 4835. If there are applicable expenses which do not fit the official categories, they can be separately entered on line 25 as "other expenses (specify)."

Personal and family living expenses, such as your own home (on the farm), garden, poultry, and livestock, are not legitimate business expenses. However, if you are an absentee landlord, and you provide a dwelling unit and some surrounding land for the personal use of your full-time *caretaker*, your expenses therewith would indeed be deductible. This is allowed by Code Section 119: Meals or Lodging Furnished for the Convenience of the Employer. The only catch is that the full-time caretaker becomes your employee. This means that you have to pay wages or other compensation (such as a share of your crops) to the caretaker, and pay a portion of his social security and medicare tax.

In the case of preproductive period expenses (where the prebearing period of any plant, vine, or tree exceeds two years), the expenditures must be capitalized. This means making entries on two different tax forms. One entry is made on Form 4835 (at line 25 in Figure 8.4) by entering the amount capitalized in parentheses. A corresponding entry is made, as a "suspense item," on Form 4562: Depreciation and Amortization. When the plant, vine, or tree becomes productive, the capitalized expenses are depreciated over the productive life of the crop-bearing item(s).

Expenses for soil and water conservation purposes, or to prevent erosion, may be deducted only if they are consistent with a plan approved by the Soil Conservation Service (SCS) of the Department of Agriculture. If not approved by the SCS or a comparable state agency, the expenditures must be capitalized similarly to preproductive period expenses above. If your conservation plan is approved, your deduction for a given year is limited to 25% of your gross rental income. If your expenses

Form 4835	FARM RENTAL INCOME AND EXPENSES				
Part II	**EXPENSES - FARM RENTAL PROPERTY**				
1	Breeding fees		15	Pension & P/S plans	
2	Chemicals		16	Rent or lease: Equipment	
3	Conservation expenses		17	Rent or lease: Other	
4	Custom hire (machine)		18	Repairs & maintenance	
5	Depreciation		19	Seeds & plants	
6	Employee benefits		20	Storage & warehousing	
7	Feed purchased		21	Supplies purchased	
8	Fertilizers & lime		22	Taxes: R.E. & other	
9	Freight & trucking		23	Utilities (& phone)	
10	Gas, fuel, & oil		24	Vet fees & medicine	
11	Insurance (NOT health)		25	Other (specify)	
12	Interest; Mortgage		/////	" "	
13	Interest; Other		/////	" "	
14	Labor hired		/////	" "	
/////	**TOTAL EXPENSES** Add all of the above ➡				

Fig. 8.4 - Complete Listing of Expense Items on Form 4835

exceed this 25% limit, the excess may be carried over to subsequent years, until used.

Most other expenses listed in Figure 8.4, we believe, are fairly self-explanatory. If not, the instructions to Form 4835 may be helpful. But in cases of honest doubt, it is best to claim the expense as appropriately as you can. Then, let the IRS comb your entries for any disallowances they may want to make.

New Vistas in Depreciation

One expense deduction in Figure 8.4 that is worthy of additional note is Depreciation (item 5). This is the same depreciation allowance that we covered in Chapter 2. The basic rules are all back there. But when applied to farming operations, new vistas open up.

There are many more classes of items to be depreciated than is the case with residential and commercial buildings in urban areas.

In typical urban rental property, the primary — and almost sole — depreciable asset is the building itself. There may be some add-on improvements, some furniture and appliances, or some pool and landscaping to depreciate, but, by and large, the building is the dominant item. In this regard, you may wish to recall Figures 2.3 and 2.4 (on pages 2-11 and 2-16).

In a farming operation, there are a great many more items to depreciate. Whereas for an urban rental there may be three depreciation schedules, for a farm rental there may be as many as 15 depreciation schedules. This greater number arises from differences in land mass to be serviced, and differences in operational functions. Whereas an urban rental may involve an acre or two at most, a farm rental may — and often does — involve hundreds and thousands of acres. Whereas an urban rental focuses primarily on its building for living and working, a farm rental focuses on its land, crops, roadways, livestock, storage facilities, machinery, equipment, etc.

Rather than trying to describe all possible forms of depreciable assets used on a farm, we present a general listing of them in Figure 8.5. As you can sense, each farm rental operation will differ with respect to specific items. Also of note is that most dwelling units on a farm are utilitarian structures in which stylish and luxurious living are unsuited. Depending on whether the depreciable items are new, used, or many years old at time of acquisition, their cost recovery periods often include all nine of the class lives listed in Figure 2.1.

There is an additional depreciation feature available to farmland owners and renters. It is an "up to" $25,000 *expense election* for depreciable assets, such as machinery and equipment, used in the farming operation. This is called the "Section 179 Expense Election." The official tax code title is: *Election to Expense Certain Depreciable Business Assets*. The term "certain" refers to tangible items (other than buildings and their structural components) which have a useful life of at least three years. The eligible items must be those which are directly associated with the landowner's share of the crops and livestock identified in the sharecropping agreement.

There are two other "expense elections" when sharecropping farmland. Section 175 allows soil and water conservation efforts to be expensed rather than capitalized. Similarly, Section 180 allows the expensing of fertilizer, lime, and marl for conditioning the land.

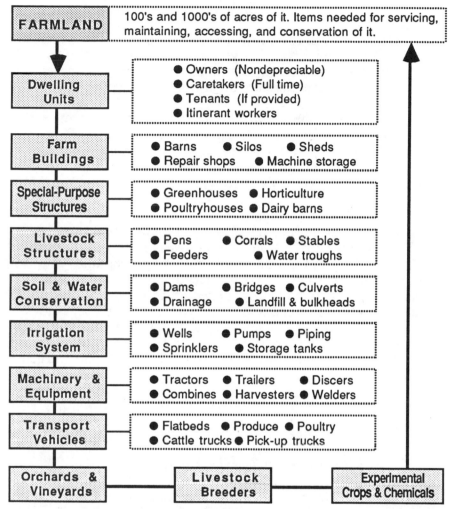

Fig. 8.5 - Multiplicity of Depreciable Assets Re Farmland Rentals

If Net Rental Loss

After subtracting the total expenses (in Figure 8.4) from the gross farm rents (in Figure 8.3), you arrive at your net farm rental income or loss. If the net figure is a loss (negative), be prepared for IRS scrutiny. Particularly so if you are an absentee landowner and some blood relative of yours in living on the property as a full-time caretaker.

Behind their wall of bureaucracy and computers, the gut reaction of most IRS examiners is that you must be a "hobby farmer." As such, the not-for-profit rules immediately apply. These rules eliminate all tax benefits that might otherwise accrue to you, as a result of the rental loss.

To meet any hobby loss arbitrariness head-on, produce your sharecropping agreement. Emphatically point to the 65% share of crops and livestock that your tenant gets. In most sharecropping situations, the tenant farmer is making his livelihood at sharecropping. He owns the machinery and drives it back and forth over vast acreages from sunup to sundown, day after day. In no way can this work be regarded as a hobby. Thus, you are the minority (35%) sharer in a full-fledged farming-for-profit endeavor.

The next stop-loss hurdle that the IRS will impose on you is a lookback at your preproductive-period expenses and your soil conservation expenses. As we described above, certain amounts of these expenses have to be capitalized. The greater the amount of capitalization the IRS can impose on you, the more your net losses are reduced. And, correspondingly, the less tax benefits you enjoy.

If you survive the above loss hurdles, Form 4835 has one more for you. At the bottom of the form there is an official instruction which reads—

> *If the result is a loss, you MUST check the box that describes your investment in this activity:*
>
> *(a)* ☐ *All investment is at risk*
> *(b)* ☐ *Some investment is not at risk*

This "must" instruction brings you back full circle to the loss limitation and at-risk rules that we discussed in detail in Chapter 5. The instruction calls your attention to Forms 6198 and 8582 and tells you to enter the amount of deductible loss in the space that we highlighted at the bottom of Figure 8.2.

If there is net rental (positive) income, Form 4835 tells you to enter the amount on Schedule E, Part V. If the net rent is a loss, Form 4835 tells you to enter the *deductible* portion of the loss also on Schedule E, Part V. Either way, you wind up back on Schedule E at its Summary (Part V). There, Form 4835 combines with other income or losses on Schedule E (Form 1040).

9

OUT-OF-STATE RENTALS

When Acquiring Rental Property Outside Your State of Domicile, Closer Attention To Tax Accounting Is Required. Stringent Travel Rules Apply; Management Contracts Involve Forms 1099-MISC (For Rents Received And Commissions Paid); Employees Necessitate Tax Withholdings (Federal, State, And Foreign). Cash Receipts Over $10,000 Are A "Must Report" On Form 8300. Co-Ownership Aggravates The Differences In State Residency Laws. Foreign Rentals Producing Net Income Invoke "Double Taxation" Treaties. To Avoid Triple Taxation, You Must Subtract From Your Resident State Return The Rental Income From Each Nonresident State.

For our purposes, the term "out-of-state" means the absentee ownership of rental realty. That is, with respect to your own primary residence, your rental property may be out-of-town, out-of-state, or out-of-country. Wherever it may be located, if the distance from your home is more than two or three hours of driving, one way, we consider that you are an absentee owner.

Absentee ownership creates special tax accounting problems of its own. What is readily tax deductible locally may not be so when out of state. Much more documentation, substantiation, and informational reporting are required. The problem can be aggravated when there are co-owners involved (other than your spouse), when various mortgage companies are involved, and when there are different tenant expectations and practices in the property area. The (tax) problems are aggravated still further should you own rental income property in a foreign country.

We do not pretend to have all of the answers and solutions to out-of-state ownership and tax problems. All we can do in this chapter is to call your attention to some of these problems and make some hopefully constructive comments thereon.

Auto and Travel

Auto and travel are a generally recognized expense deduction with respect to owning and managing rental property. If the property is located in your immediate neighborhood or only a few miles away, allowable auto expenses are simply a standard mileage rate of about 30 cents per business mile. That is, provided you keep a business mileage log. You keep track of your trips to and from the property, to and from hardware and supply stores, and to and from the bank with your rent collections. Under these circumstances, it is unlikely that you would run up more than 500 to 1,000 rental miles for the year.

Now, suppose your property is located 500 to 1,000 miles or more away. Would you go there two or three times a month to do the gardening, sweep the pool, and pick up the rent checks? How often would you go to do ordinary repairs or to supply the tenant with small tools and supplies?

The minute your rental property is more than several hundred miles, one way, your trip expenses take on the nature of *travel*. Then, more stringent tax rules apply. The term "travel" means away from home overnight. Travel is necessary when the property is so far distant that it would be imprudent to go and return within a normal workday.

The stringency of the travel rules requires adequate substantiation of each trip undertaken. On this particular point, Code Section 274(d) reads in part as—

No deduction or credit shall be allowed—
(1) under sections 162 [relating to trade or business expenses] or 212 [relating to expenses for production of income] for any traveling expenses (including meals and lodging while away from home) . . . unless the taxpayer substantiates by adequate records . . . (A) the amount of such expense or other item, (B) the time and place of travel, [and] (C) the

business purpose of the expense or other item. [Emphasis added.]

In other words, for out-of-state (out-of-town or out-of-country) visits to your property, you have to justify each trip. If your property is 1,500 miles away, say, and you visit it regularly once a year to inspect it, arrange locally for repairs and maintenance, renew the rental lease, and so on — and you document all items therewith — your expenses generally would be allowable. This is because Section 212 says—

In the case of an individual, there shall be allowed as a deduction all the ordinary and necessary expenses paid or incurred during the taxable year—
    (1) for the production or collection of income;
    (2) for the management, conservation, or maintenance of property held for the production of income.

But if you visited your out-of-state property more than once a year, you had better have a good and compelling reason. Be prepared to explain why you could not use the telephone, express mail, or fax machine.

Local Management Contract

Assuming there are no family members in the vicinity of your out-of-state property who could look after it for you, what recourse do you have for avoiding second or third trips?

One recourse is to engage a local property manager or management firm. Such a manager could collect the rent, see that all ordinary repairs were made, pay all local operating expenses (such as utilities, fees, gardening, trash removal, etc.), and occasionally visit the premises to verify that no illegal activities are taking place there. All of these matters and others should be set forth in a written management contract.

The management contract should specify that the property manager is not your employee. He is an independent contractor on his own. He should have his own place of business and not live on your premises (unless he pays full rent). The presumption is that he is managing other properties than yours.

You require the property manager to set up a separate trust account (checking only, at a bank) in your behalf. Do not allow him to commingle your money matters with those of others whose property he may be managing. You require him to deposit the monthly rents collected, pay himself the agreed commission, and pay all operating and maintenance expenses. Have him receive all tenant complaints and report to you only if necessary. Require that he provide you a quarterly statement showing the year-to-date rent receipts and disbursements paid. The IRS will generally accept these statements as documentary evidence of the applicable entries on your Schedule E.

To keep your hand on the overall management, *you* make the monthly mortgage payments, semi-annual property taxes, and annual insurance premiums. These are matters which are usually handled through the mail anyhow. As the property owner, you are legally responsible for their payment, no matter what.

IRS Form 1099-MISC

As an out-of-state rental property owner, you should become familiar with IRS Form 1099-MISC. Its official title is: **Statement for Recipients of Miscellaneous Income**. It is referred to in the Internal Revenue Code as an "information return." This is because it contains (tax accountable) information concerning transactions with other persons. More to the point, Form 1099-MISC is a "you-report-on-me-and-I-report-on-you" return.

To introduce Form 1099-MISC to you, we present Figure 9.1. It is an edited version, necessarily. It consists of 12 numbered boxes with dollar signs on each one. Only two of the boxes — Box 1: *Rents* and Box 7: *Nonemployee compensation* — are of direct interest to the subject at hand.

In the case of a property manager collecting your rents, what do you suppose he is going to do?

He is going to prepare a 1099-MISC, reporting to the IRS in Box 1 the amount of gross rents that he collected for you during the year. He has to report the gross: not the net. Otherwise, he is subject to an IRS penalty. He, of course, is required to send you a copy of that which he sends to the IRS.

What do you suppose is the purpose of reporting your gross rents to the IRS?

Answer: Back to Schedule E, to the line which reads *Rents received*. When you report your rents on Schedule E, the IRS will computer-match this with what the property manager reports.

PAYER Name & Address	1. Rents	FORM 1099 - MISC
	2.	Statement for recipients of
	3.	**Miscellaneous** **Income**
Payer's Fed. I.D.No.	Payee's Soc.Sec.No.	4.
PAYEE Name & Address	5.	6.
	7. Nonemployee Compensation	8.
	9.	10.
	11.	12.

Copy A : for IRS	Copy 2 : for State	Copy B : for Payee	Copy C : for Payer

Fig. 9.1 - Edited Version of Information Form 1099 - MISC

Switching hats around for a moment, do you have to report on the property manager?

Yes, you do. You have to report to the IRS, in Box 7 of a separate Form 1099-MISC, the amount of gross commission you paid to the property manager. This will be the total commissions (remuneration) that your property manager took out of your trust account in his own behalf. You have to do this if you want an expense deduction on Schedule E for the commissions paid.

On this specific point, Section 6041A(a): *Returns Regarding Remuneration for Services*, reads in part as—

If (1) any service-recipient engaged in a trade or business pays in the course of such trade or business during any calendar year remuneration to any person for services performed by such person, and (2) the aggregate of such remuneration paid to such person during the calendar year is $600 or more, then the service-recipient shall make a return, according to the forms or regulations prescribed by the [IRS]. [Emphasis added.]

Employing a Resident Manager

If you own an apartment or commercial complex out-of-state, and you have ten or more rental units, we urge you to consider employing a resident manager. Provide a dwelling unit for said manager and require that he accept it as part of his employment contract. With 10, 20, 30 or more tenants in and out of your property daily, you want someone on your premises 24 hours a day. This is too much to expect from an independent property manager, who has other properties to oversee.

The usual practice in resident management is to employ a husband and wife as a pair. Typically, the wife manages the office, answers phone calls, collects the rents, pays the bills, places ads regarding vacancies, and keeps the books. The husband does the yard work, general maintenance, ordinary repairs, patchups and painting, and moving of furniture and equipment, and supervises any local repairmen (plumbers, electricians, carpenters, glaziers, etc.) who are called to the premises.

To make the arrangement more effective, prepare a written contract for the resident management pair. Set forth their duties and the amount of compensation to each. Base the compensation on a weekly or monthly rate rather than hourly. You want at least one of them available at all times.

Each spouse of the management pair becomes a separate employee of yours. As such, you are responsible for withholding income taxes (federal *and* state), social security taxes (federal only), and disability taxes (state only). For these withholding purposes, you have to apply to the IRS for an Employer Identification Number: Form SS-4. Then you have to prepare Employer Quarterly Returns (federal and state), make tax deposits, prepare Forms W-2, and so on. We suggest that you contact your bookkeeper, accountant, or tax advisor regarding these matters.

As the employer of a husband and wife resident manager pair, you do have to provide them opportunity for a regular vacation period: two weeks or whatever. During their vacation, you need to make provision for a "relief manager." For this, select one of your more reliable tenants and give him/her/them two weeks' "free rent" for their substitutional effort. A relief manager is not expected to do the same work as the regular manager. The relief primarily answers the phone, takes messages, holds the rent checks, observes the goings-on, and — if need be — contacts you in emergencies.

Don't worry about having to report the free rent as income to the relief manager. As we covered in Chapter 6 (Vacation Home Rentals), two weeks is de minimis rental use requiring no inclusion as taxable income.

Don't worry about the dwelling unit being furnished to the regular manager, either. It is not reportable income. For this, you can rely on Section 119(a): Meals and Lodging Furnished to

Employee, His Spouse, and His Dependents Pursuant to Employment. This section reads in principal part as—

There shall be excluded from gross income of an employee the value of any meals or lodging furnished to him, his spouse, or any of his dependents . . . if— the employee is required to accept such lodging on the business premises of his employer as a condition of his employment.

As to the gross wages that you pay to the husband and wife management pair, you get an expense deduction on your Schedule E. You also get an expense deduction for your share of the social security and medicare taxes that you are required to pay on behalf of the management pair.

Local Consultants on Tap

Even with an on-site manager, there inevitably will arise particular problems which require professional expertise that your manager cannot handle. For example, one of your tenants is discovered dealing drugs and laundering money. He pays rent to the manager in cash. Not only that, he pays the rent two or three months at a time, in advance. Your manager tells you about this. When he does, you have a scary legal problem on your hands.

Once you accept drug money in payment for a legitimate service that you have rendered, and you know about it, all of your money — whether commingled with the drug money or not — is treated as "tainted." Under federal law (and some state laws), your property could be seized as part of the drug ring and money-laundering scheme. Obviously, you need to make immediate contact with a local attorney or other consultant familiar with such matters.

In any business activity, unforeseen events and unforeseen needs will arise. To prepare for these eventualities, you should have on tap at least three types of professional consultants. In your ready files, you should have the name, address, and phone number of—

1. An attorney
   — specializing in real estate and tenant law
2. An accountant
   — specializing in nonresident tax matters
3. A realtor
   — specializing in property exchanges and market trends.

On your next once-a-year visit to your property, personally contact one or more of each type to establish a rapport and the scope of his expertise. Whatever you pay these persons, currently or in the future, is an expense deduction on your Schedule E.

To give you some perspective of the kind of matters that you might submit to the local consultants, we present Figure 9.2. As implied therein, you should keep your manager informed of the consultants that you have selected. Authorize him to contact them on his own, should he be unable to contact you in a hurry.

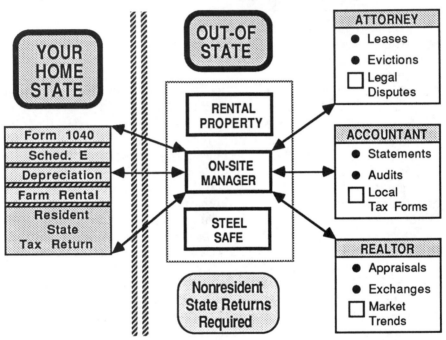

Fig. 9.2 - Likely Needs for Out-of-State Consultants

Another Expense: Security Safe

The ownership and management of out-of-state property requires another expenditure which you might not incur for property readily accessible to you. This is an adequately-sized steel safe, with combination lock. That is, provided you have a resident manager with a separate office on site. Have the safe located in an office which can be isolated from the manager's dwelling unit. We showed this separation in Figure 9.2.

Direct the manager (in his employment contract) to store in the safe all cash, rent receipts, security deposits, valuables (including those for tenants), bank statements, spare checks, spare keys, and so on. You never know when some irate tenant, vandal, or armed robber will enter your premises and make demands. This is especially likely once it becomes known in the property area that the owner lives in another state.

Even in the normal course of tenant activities, there could be some unusual requests for safekeeping favors. Consider, for example, that one of your tenants is a route salesman and delivery person for a national franchiser. Many of his customers pay in cash (strictly legitimate). At month's end, he has collected $10,500 in green paper cash. The banks are closed for a few days. So the tenant asks your manager to store the cash in your safe, and tips the manager $100 for doing so.

Are there any tax reporting consequences?

You bet there are!

The good book (IR Code) at Section 6050I says—

(a) Cash Receipts of More Than $10,000
Any person (1) who is engaged in a trade or business, and (2) who, in the course of such trade or business, receives more than $10,000 in cash in 1 transaction (or 2 or more related transactions), shall make the return described in subsection (b).

Subsection (b) describes IRS **Form 8300**: Report of Cash Payments Over $10,000 Received in a Trade or Business. The form requires identifying the individual having the cash, the nature of the transaction, the exact amount (in $100 bills, foreign currency, traveler's checks, or coins), and the date and place of the transaction.

Naturally, your manager does not have a pad of Form 8300s on hand. So he puts the money in the safe and contacts the local tax consultant that you have designated.

The cost of buying and installing the security safe on your business premises is a Section 179 (tangible property) expenditure. It is fully deductible — up to $25,000 by the way — on Schedule E. We mentioned the Section 179 expense option in Chapter 8 (Farmland Rentals) on page 8-14.

Co-Ownership Accounting

Here's a situation that commonly occurs. Two business associates (and their spouses) get along well. They have the same investment interests and expertise. They decide to acquire a rental complex in another state where the economy is currently slow, but has great recovery potential. They pool their funds and buy an 8-unit rental building. They engage a property manager who also manages other properties in the area. The property is titled tenants in common: 62%-38%. You are the 62% owner.

You live in State A; the 38% owner is in State B; the property is located in State C. What are the principal tax accounting features that will affect each co-owner's Schedule E (1040)?

As starters, both co-owners instruct the property manager to open a trust account with a local bank, in both names. Require a *checking-only* account so as to avoid the computer complications of interest being earned and being reported to the IRS (on whose social security number?). Require the manager to deposit all rents, security deposits, and other money collections, and pay all operating expenses, including property taxes, property insurance, and his commissions. Exclude mortgage payments (for reasons given below). Also require the manager to provide each of you with a quarterly statement and a year-end statement based on a 100% operation.

Request the property manager to contact a local tax preparation service, subject to both co-owners' approval. Have that service prepare **two** statements: a 62% statement and a 38% statement — of income, expenses, *and* depreciation. You'll need to supply the property acquisition cost papers, the property assessment values, and the title deed showing each co-owner's percent of ownership. Have the tax service also prepare two separate 1099 forms for rents received and two separate 1099 forms for commissions paid.

Why are two separate tax statements — 62% and 38% — needed?

Answer: To satisfy the IRS's computer-matching mania. Each co-owner's Schedule E and other matters on his Form 1040 must stand alone. Since each resides in a different state, each is subject to being contacted by a different IRS center and by different state revenue agencies. There is no reason whatsoever for the 62% owner to drag in the 38% owner . . . or vice versa.

The endless harangue of IRS's computer matching can be visualized, we think, from our presentation in Figure 9.3. It usually

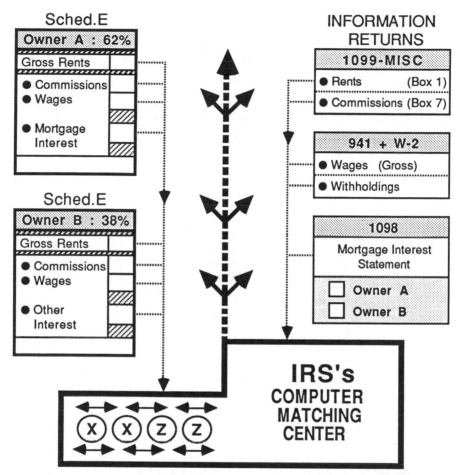

Fig. 9.3 - Computer Matching of Co-Owners' Schedules E

takes up to 18 months after a return is filed before the IRS computer cross-matches the "1099" information. Each co-owner's return is computer identified by his/her own separate social security number. Separate rental property income and expense statements, as above, can keep the tax problems of one co-owner from intruding into the tax return of the other co-owner.

Unfortunately, there is one predicament in our Figure 9.3 presentation. It's the matter of mortgage interest proration between co-owners. The IRS requires each mortgagee to report to it on

Form 1098: Mortgage Interest Statement, the total interest received on each loan outstanding. The mortgagee is required to send only one Form 1098 per loan, regardless of the number of co-signers and co-owners involved. For the 62/38 arrangement above, no mortgagee will prepare two Forms 1098: one for 62% interest paid; one for 38% interest paid. Thus, you have a problem.

The way around this problem is for each co-owner to write a separate check monthly for his share of the mortgage payment. The 62% owner collects the 38% owner's check, and mails both checks at the same time. The 62% owner then instructs the mortgage company to show *both* names on the one Form 1098, but with only the 62% owner's social security number. Most mortgagees will at least do this.

At Schedule E filing time, the 62% owner enters his share of the total Form 1098 interest on the line with reads: *Mortgage interest, etc.* The 38% owner enters his share (on his Schedule E) at the next line below which reads: *Other interest.* The "mortgage interest" line is computer matched, whereas the "other interest" line is not computer matched. As long as the mortgage interest line is less than what the mortgagee reports, the IRS computer is happy.

What About Foreign Rentals?

Suppose that, for whatever reason or circumstance, you acquire rental real estate in a foreign country. The country has its own tax and property laws. It doesn't give a hoot about U.S. tax laws or the IRS's computer. You own property in that country, so you obey its laws. Fair enough? Does this cause you any additional tax accounting problems?

For federal returns — Form 1040 and attachments — the answer is essentially "No."

As a U.S. taxpayer, whether you acquire rental property in Canada, South America, Europe, or Asia, you report your rental income and expenses on Schedule E. There will be some additional taxes and expenses (such as travel and foreign currency exchanges) but otherwise you Schedule E-treat the property as though it were located next door to your primary residence.

In case you have any doubt about this, and believe in some of the "tax haven" fairy tales that you might have heard, we want to apprise you of IR Code Sections 61 and 862. For brevity, we quote only the pertinent portions of these two sections for you.

Section 61: *Gross Income Defined*, reads—

> Except as otherwise provided . . . gross income means all
> income *from whatever source derived,* including (but not
> limited to) the following items:
>   *(5) Rents.* [Emphasis added.]

There is a total of 15 specific items of income asserted under the
jurisdiction of the U.S., no matter where the source of income may
be. It can be anyplace in the world . . . or the universe!

Section 862: *Gross Income from Sources Without the
United States,* reads—

> *(a) The following items of gross income shall be treated as
> income from sources without the United States:*
>   *(4) rentals or royalties from property located without the
>   United States or from any interest in such property . . .*
> *(b) From the items of gross income specified in subsection (a)
> there shall be deducted the expenses, losses, and other
> deductions* **properly apportioned or allocated thereto.**
> [Emphasis added.]

The phrase: "properly apportioned or allocated thereto" has a
special meaning with regard to foreign rentals. If you travel to a
foreign country to check on the condition of your property and
renew its management contract, and you take some vacation time
while there, you have to apportion the total trip expenses between
your business activities and those which are nonbusiness.

If you pay to a foreign agency the functional equivalent of a
property tax, be it called a capital tax, value added tax, ownership
tax, social tax, or other, it is fully deductible on your Schedule E.
However, this is **not** the case in the event of a foreign tax on your
net rental income. The consequence is that you are subject to *double
taxation* on the same income. Unless there is a U.S. tax treaty with
the foreign country where your property is located, you get no relief
from this double taxation.

Foreign Tax Treaties

The U.S. has tax treaties with about 45 of the 175 sovereign
countries of the world. The carrot idea behind these tax treaties is to
provide a credit, against the U.S. tax, for "double taxation" on the
same income. The means for doing so is by filing **Form 1116:**
Foreign Tax Credit, and attaching it to your Form 1040.

Form 1116 has appropriate check-boxes for classifying the type of income that is double taxed. Those pertinent to our discussion are:

☐ Passive income   (such as from rental real estate)
☐ Interest income   (such as from bank deposits)
☐ Financial income   (such as from capital gains)

The form requires that the tax paid on this income be reported in foreign currency, and then converted to U.S. currency. The conversion date is the tax due date (or date paid, if earlier) in the foreign situs country.

The net result from the Form 1116 computations is that only a **limited portion** of the actual foreign tax paid becomes an offsetting credit against the U.S. tax.

There is a more pervasive — perhaps perverted — reason behind the 45 foreign tax treaties. It is to "exchange information" on U.S. taxpayers investing in the signatory countries. It is an extension of Big Brother's long arm into the financial affairs of U.S. taxpayers abroad. In every U.S. Consulate Office in the world, there is an IRS representative whose function is to canvass the area for U.S. persons having bank accounts and investments there. This is so dictated by Section 7601(a) of the IR Code.

Many countries resent this IRS intrusion into their sovereign affairs. So much so that approximately 130 nations have not entered into a tax treaty with the U.S.

One such country, for example, is Uruguay. This South American country borders on the Atlantic Ocean between Brazil and Argentina (neither of which has a tax treaty with the U.S.). Uruguay has a population of about three million persons, mostly of European descent. It encourages foreign investment, and has no foreign exchange controls. Capital is free to enter or leave Uruguay, subject only to its tax laws. It imposes an Industry and Commerce Income Tax (ICIT) and a Capital and Net Worth Tax (CNWT), among others. The ICIT applies to the net income from rental property; the CNWT applies to account balances in Uruguayan banks. The ICIT rate is 30%; the CNWT rate is about 3% for individuals.

Suppose you were to buy a 2-bedroom rental unit in a high-rise condominium in Punta del Este, Uruguay. This is an up-scale beach-front resort area, where peak season rents fetch as much as

$6,000 U.S. per month. This is positive net income property, after all applicable expenses. Foreign investors worldwide acquire the rental units through local real estate and property management firms. As a U.S. taxpayer acquiring such a unit, what would your tax options be?

Obviously, you can always choose to pay double income taxes: to the U.S. *and* to Uruguay. Since Uruguay has no tax treaty with the U.S., Form 1116 (foreign tax credit) would not apply.

Another way would be to ignore Schedule E (for the Uruguay property) and open up a bank account there. Instruct the Uruguayan bank to automatically transfer all funds in excess of $9,999 to your U.S. bank. Then, when you prepare Form 1040, answer "Yes" to the foreign bank accounts question on Schedule B, Part III. Follow the instructions thereto and prepare **Form TD F 90-22.1**: Report of Foreign Bank and Financial Accounts. Check the box:

Maximum value ☐ *Under $10,000.*

This tells the IRS that you are not engaged in drug trafficking or other illegal activities.

Prepare Uruguayan ICIT and CNWT tax returns and pay that tax promptly. This gives you a valid reason for visiting Punta del Este at least once a year. If you vacation there for 14 days or less, you do not trigger the U.S. vacation home rental rules (in Chapter 6). Of course, you pay U.S. tax on your U.S. bank earnings.

State-of-Residence Adjustments

As a U.S. taxpayer, you probably reside in at least one of the 50 states of the union. You prepare and file a resident income tax return for that state. But what about your out-of-state rental property? Do you pay tax to your state of domicile on that property?

Yes, you can . . . and will. You may pay, in effect, a "triple tax" unless you make proper adjustments on your resident state return. You certainly should expect to pay tax in the nonresident state for any property located there.

Most states in the U.S. honor the sovereignty of other states (domestic and foreign) over all real and tangible property within their jurisdictional borders. California is more high handed than other states. It wants to tax you on your worldwide and U.S.-wide income, just like the federal. Yet, California totally lacks legal taxing jurisdiction over rental property in Florida, Mexico, or

Oregon, for example. To minimize any triple taxing effect, you have to specifically identify your nonresident source income and "back it off" of your resident tax return . . . if you can.

Most income-taxing states today piggy-back the federal Form 1040. All such states insist that you attach a complete copy of your federal return. You are then permitted to claim a *partial credit* for the income tax you paid to another state. But what about the nine non-income-taxing states? You have a dilemma. Suppose, for example, you live in California and have rental property in Florida. (Florida, by the way, is a no-income-tax state.) The property provides net rental income: not a loss. Should you pay California tax on the Florida property income?

Common sense suggests: Certainly not. But California gives you no choice. As a California resident, you must pay tax to California on your Florida property income. This is because there is no "other state" tax paid on the same income (for which a partial credit might be claimed). This means using your own ingenuity on your California return, especially its **Schedule CA (540)**. You might try making an entry in its subtraction column under *other income, describe*. To be above board about it, make a notation such as—

Non California source income: Florida rental real estate: Property "C," Schedule E (Form 1040) $_____.

Now, consider the other way around. You reside in Florida (or Texas, which is also a non-income-taxing state) and you have rental property in California. You had better file a California nonresident return, and report your net rental income or loss there. When the time comes to sell said property, your tax situation becomes disastrous. California taxes nonresidents on the "gross-up" principle. This means that you pay a nonresident tax to California at the *high end* of your California-equivalent federal adjusted gross income. California is one of the nastiest states of all in its treatment of nonresidents and residents with out-of-state property.

10

SECTION 1031 EXCHANGES

There Is Potential Nonrecognition (Non-Taxability) Of Capital Gain If Rental Properties Are Traded In A "Like-Kind" Exchange. To Make An Exchange Work, "Boot" Is Required In The Form Of Cash And Noncash (Nonlike Property). Said Boot Is Determined By EQUITY BALANCING The FMVs Of The Like Properties. All Real Estate Exchanges Are Broker Reported To The IRS On Form 1099-S. You, In Turn, Report Your Exchange Computations On Form 8824. Any Recognized Gain On Form 8824 Goes Onto Form 4797, Where It Combines With Other Gain/Loss Transactions.

One of the great tax excitements in the real estate world is the exchanging of property under Section 1031. Such exchanging is commonly referred to as *nontaxable exchanges*. It is the reference to "nontaxable" that excites long-term property owners.

Many property owners construe the word "nontaxable" as being tax-free. They envision the exchanging of realty, property-for-property, year after year, throughout their entire lives and paying no tax — ever — thereon. This paying-no-tax syndrome arises from the capital gain in property which, under the right exchange conditions, can be postponed. Tax recognition of the capital gain can be postponed and re-postponed as often as a property owner likes. There is no limitation on the number of Section 1031 exchanges that can be made in a lifetime.

Sooner or later, though, tax on the postponed capital gain **will be** paid. As a frequent exchanger, it will be paid either by you, your estate, or your heirs. It may be paid partially by you in down-exchanges and in nonlike exchanges. When paid by your estate, it is called a death tax (or succession tax) instead of a capital gain tax. This change of tax character in an estate often misleads property owners into believing that the capital gain tax — via perpetual exchanging — may never be paid. This simply is not true.

Nonetheless, exchanging properties, under the rules of Section 1031, opens up a wide range of planning options with regard to the disposition of rental property. In this chapter, therefore, we want to stress the core features of Section 1031 and some (not all) of the IRS regulations therewith. We also want to acquaint you with three particular IRS forms (namely: Form 1099-S, Form 8824, and Form 4797) that will lock you into its computer-tracking program.

Must Be "Like-Kind"

A fully nontaxable exchange is a transaction in which the value of the property received is equal to or greater than the value of the property conveyed. In addition, the two properties must be solely of like-kind. This raises the question: What is meant by "like-kind"?

Properties are of like-kind if they are of the same nature, class, or character. Comparability of size, grade, or quality has no bearing on the likeness issue. Properties are of like-kind if their basic attributes are similar in nature. Real estate is actually the easiest example to portray.

The basic characteristic of real estate is its *appurtenant land.* Whether it is improved land (with buildings, structures, etc.) or unimproved land (raw and in its pristine state), its inherent nature is the same. Land is an asset of long duration which is nondepreciable. The extent of any improvements thereto addresses its grade or quality (and hence its value), but not its kind or class. This means that a residential rental (with its appurtenant land) exchanged for acres of bare land would qualify as like-kind. Regulation 1.1031(a)-1(b) supports this improved-unimproved land likeness.

To be of like-kind, the ownership interests in the land exchanged must also be similar in legal nature. That is, if the owner of the land conveyed has fee simple rights to that land, the land received must also be fee simple or comparable thereto. (The term "fee simple," recall, means absolute ownership of land with unrestricted rights of disposition.) If the land received has restrictions on its disposition, such as life estate, irrevocable lease, or leasehold interest for less than 30 years, the legal rights to that land are not the same as fee simple. However, the IRS has ruled [Rev. Rul. 78-72, 1978-1 CB 258] that where the initial term of a leasehold on land is 30 years or more, and the leasehold itself has no separate capital value, such leasehold land would qualify as like-kind to fee simple.

This like-kindness of land for real estate exchanges rules out the exchanging of a rental mobile home (on rented land) for a fixed residential rental, or a batch of farm machinery for some bare land. Unless the properties exchanged are *solely* of like-kind, nonlike properties constitute a "tax-now" transaction.

Section 1031 Overview

For exchanging rental real estate, Section 1031 is the tax law on point. Its official heading in the IR Code is: ***Exchange of Property Held for Productive Use or Investment***. This heading alone targets the prerequisites for the types of real estate that can be exchanged tax-free (at the time of the exchange).

For nontaxable exchanges, the prerequisites are EITHER that—

1. The property be held for productive use, OR
2. The property be held for investment.

Rental real estate qualifies in both cases. It is held for productive use in that it produces rental income which is subject to ordinary tax. It is also held for investment purposes in that it generally appreciates in value over time. This appreciation produces investment gain which is subject to capital gain tax. It is the capital gain tax that is the object of postponement in a Section 1031 exchange.

Section 1031 has eight separate subsections, some of which have sub-subsections of their own. For overview purposes, we present in Figure 10.1 the headings to all of the subsections and sub-subsections. Skimming down the listing in Figure 10.1 gives you a quick insight into what is pertinent and what is not pertinent, relative to rental real estate.

A rule directed especially at realty owners is subsection (h). Its heading is: ***Special Rule for Foreign Real and Personal Property***. Subsection 1031(h)(1) reads in full as—

INTERNAL REVENUE CODE	
Chapter 1	Normal Taxes and Surtaxes
Subchapter O	Gain or Loss on Disposition of Property
Part III	Common Nontaxable Exchanges
Sec. 1031	Exchange of Property Held for Productive Use or Investment

Subsection		Heading & Subheading (some abbreviated)
(a)		Nonrecognition of Gain: Exchanges Solely In Kind
	(1)	In General
	(2)	Exceptions
	(3)	Requirement for Identification & Completion: 180 Days
(b)		Gain from Exchanges Not Solely in Kind
(c)		Loss from Exchanges Not Solely in Kind
(d)		Basis
(e)		Echanges of Livestock of Different Sexes
(f)		Exchanges Between Related Persons
	(1)	In General
	(2)	Certain Dispositions Not Taken into Account
	(3)	Related Person
	(4)	Treatment of Certain Transactions
(g)		Special Rule: Substantial Diminution of Risk
	(1)	In General
	(2)	Property to Which Subsection Applies
(h)		Special Rule for Foreign Real Property

Fig. 10.1 - Subsections and Sub-subsections of Section 1031

For purposes of this section [1031], real property located in the United States and real property located outside the United States are not property of a like kind.

Subsection 1031(h) is unequivocal. If you own foreign realty (as we discussed in the latter part of Chapter 9), you cannot make a 1031 exchange for comparable property in the U.S. . . . or vice versa. The reasons should be obvious. For you, your legal rights to land in a foreign country will differ from those in the U.S. Secondly, if you were allowed to nontaxably exchange foreign property for U.S. property, there is a possibility that you could avoid altogether any U.S. tax on the capital gain. As we said earlier, in a 1031 exchange, the tax is postponed; it is not forgiven.

The Core Statute

The key wording for property exchanges under Section 1031 is its subsection (a), paragraph (1). This core statute reads as—

> (a) **Nonrecognition of Gain or Loss From Exchanges Solely in Kind—**
> *(1) In general — No gain or loss shall be recognized on the exchange of property held for productive use in a trade or business or for investment if such property is exchanged solely for property of like kind which is to be held either for productive use in a trade or business or for investment.*

For realty exchanges, this wording is precise and specific. It says nothing whatever about an exchange being "nontaxable," "tax-free," or "tax postponed." It says—

No gain or loss shall be recognized . . . IF—

In tax jargon, the term "recognized" means tax recognized and therefore taxable. The inverse, nonrecognized (or nonrecognition), means not taxable . . . "if."

The core key is: There is no tax consequence (at the time) IF the exchange is *solely* of like-kind. One of the conditions for this like-kindness is the statutory wording itself. The use of the property before the exchange — either productively or for investment — must continue with the replacement property after the exchange. That is, you cannot use Section 1031 to avoid tax on a transaction, and then, after the transaction is over, convert the property received into nonproductive/non-investment use.

Dealers in real estate, subdividers of land, and developers of property are barred from engaging in Section 1031 exchanges on their own behalf. They may, however, participate as a "straw party" between two unrelated exchangers who separately own the productive/investment property exchanged.

Money & Nonlike Property

A Section 1031 exchange may consist of part taxable and part nontaxable. As long as at least two like-kind properties change hands, money and nonlike property may be thrown in to sweeten the deal. This is called "boot." The portion of the exchange represented by money and nonlike property must be clearly ascertained. That portion is taxable. It is taxable to the recipient of the boot.

Incidentally, money is not treated as property of any kind. Money is a unit of measure of value: the dollar. To at least some degree, money is required in every transaction. It is required, if for no other reason, to pay the expenses of the exchange and to pay commissions to the exchange brokers. Money may be in the form of cash (green paper), personal check, money order, traveler's check(s), "plastic" money, personal loans, and mortgage loans.

Nonlike property may be items of value which the parties to the exchange are willing to include. All nonlike property must be assigned a specific market value. Normally, professional appraisers are helpful in establishing fair market values that are acceptable to the parties involved.

Here's a simple example of nonlike property included in an exchange. The like-kind properties are rental realty for rental realty (or farmland for farmland). Included in the deal is a pleasure boat and trailer camper. Obviously, the boat and camper are the nonlike properties.

Another medium used in exchanges is debt relief and debt assumption. That is, one party assumes the debt of another party. Or, the parties may swap their debts associated with the properties exchanged. All debts have a determinable monetary value at time of the exchange.

In a Section 1031 transaction, the total value of like property, money, and nonlike property on one side of the exchange must equal that on the other side. In other words, the economic positions of the parties before and after the exchange must remain the same. Not tax positions: just the economic positions. The tax positions of the exchanging parties have no relationship to each other.

Market value equality must be the same on both sides of an exchange. After all, no one with a $135,000 piece of property is going to exchange it for a $123,000 piece of property and be happy about it. The $135,000 owner wants money and other property added to the $123,000 property to come up to his $135,000. Thus, there is need for $12,000 in "boot" (123,000 + 12,000 = 135,000). It is rare indeed for two like-kind properties offered in exchange to be exactly equal in value. Consequently, the use of money and nonlike property are the rule: not the exception.

Equity Balance: Step 1

We used the phrase "market value equality" above because it is easier to comprehend initially. For tax accounting purposes, however, the exchange equation is an *equity balance*: not a market balance. The term "equity" in real estate, as you know, is market value minus mortgage indebtedness. Even when the market values are in balance, the equities in the properties exchanged may not be.

Consider, for example, two properties A and Z each worth $150,000. Property A has a mortgage balance on it of $50,000; Property Z has a mortgage balance of $85,000. The equities in each of these properties are:

```
Property A:  $150,000 - 50,000  =  $100,000
Property Z:  $150,000 - 85,000  =     65,000
              Equity imbalance   =  $ 35,000
```

If you are Owner A, are you willing to swap a $50,000 mortgage to take on an $85,000 mortgage, just because the two market values are the same?

Of course you would not do so. There's an equity imbalance of $35,000. Either you get $35,000 cash or other (nonlike) property out of the deal, or there is no deal.

Equity balancing is required, regardless of the number of properties involved in the exchange. Section 1031 does not limit the exchange to one property for one property, or one owner to one owner. Multiple properties and multiple owners may be — and frequently are — involved. This is one of the really attractive strategic features of Section 1031 exchanges.

As Owner A, you may exchange your property for two properties B and C. Each of these two properties may be owned by entirely separate parties. Although multi-property exchanges are more complex, there still has to be an equity balance. On one side of the balancing scales is property (or properties) *conveyed*. On the other side is the property (or properties) *received*. The total equity conveyances and total equity receipts must balance.

To illustrate, let's assume that you convey a single property worth $365,000. In exchange, you receive two properties whose total worth is $300,000. All three properties have mortgages on them, as exemplified in Figure 10.2. Note that you receive "boot" out of the deal because your equity in Property A is $30,000 greater than the combined equities of B and C. The boot is allocated

Step 1	EQUITY BALANCE WITH "BOOT"			
	Property A	Properties Received		
Item	Conveyed	B	C	Total
FMV *	$365,000	$130,000	$170,000	$300,000
Mortgage Debt	<285,000>	<100,000>	<150,000>	<250,000>
Actual Equity	80,000	30,000	20,000	50,000
Boot Required				
● Cash	——	4,700	5,300	10,000
● Other	——	——	20,000	20,000
Balanced Equity	80,000	34,700○	45,300□	80,000

* FMV = Fair Market Value.   "Other" at FMV.

○ = 130 / 300 x $80,000 = 34,700   □ = 170 / 300 x $80,000 = 45,300

Fig. 10.2 - Equity Balance to Determine Amount of "Boot" Required

between properties B and C in proportion to their fair market values (FMV). For illustration purposes, we show, in Figure 10.2, $20,000 of boot as other than like-kind property.

In any 1031 exchange, Figure 10.2 is the essential "Step 1" for understanding what takes place in an exchange. With this in mind, you may want to study Figure 10.2 more carefully. It embodies a basic and fundamental principle: the determination of the amount of boot. We use Figure 10.2 later in a comprehensive example.

The exchange broker handling the deal is not going to explain to you the mechanics of equity balancing and boot determination. The title company (or companies) involved is not going to explain it to you either. And the IRS is certainly not going to explain it to you. In all likelihood, *you* will have to explain it to the IRS. They will be looking strictly for the "boot" so they can tax you accordingly.

Taxability of "Boot"

The term "boot" does not appear in Section 1031 anywhere. What you find are subsections (b) and (c), each using the common phrase: *not solely in kind*. Embodied in these two subsections is such wording as "other property or money." Here, "other" means nonlike. It is safe to conclude, therefore, that "boot" is synonymous with money (cash) and/or other (nonlike) property.

Subsection (b): *Gain from Exchange Not Solely in Kind*, reads in pertinent part as follows:

> *If an exchange . . . consists not only of property permitted by [subsection (a)], but also of other property or money, then the gain, if any, to the recipient shall be recognized, but in an amount not in excess of the sum of such money and the fair market value of such other property.* [Emphasis added.]

What is Section 1031(b) really saying?

It says that if the boot received is $50,000, for example, and the gain realized on the transaction is $90,000, for example, the entire amount of the boot is taxed. But if the gain realized is $30,000, for example, only $30,000 of the $50,000 boot is taxed.

Consider, now, the opposite situation: loss instead of gain. Subsection (c): *Loss from Exchange Not Solely in Kind*, reads in pertinent part:

> *If an exchange . . . consists not only of property permitted by [subsection (a)], but also of other property or money, then no loss from the exchange shall be recognized.*

In other words, Section 1031(c) says that even if boot is received, and there is a bona fide tax loss resulting from the exchange, the loss is *not* tax recognized. The loss is not a loss forever, however. It is carried over to the tax basis of the property received in the exchange, recoverable when said property is subsequently sold.

Adjusted Basis: Step 2

One of the most unsatisfying points to get across to aggressive property owners is the importance of adjusted basis in the property they are about to exchange. By an "aggressive" property owner, we mean one who has refinanced his rental property several times, deliberately keeping his equity therein to a minimum. In most cases, the refinanced money is used to acquire other property or is spent on personal living wants. Except for the direct cost of the refinancings (loan points, title fees, etc.), and any expenditures for direct improvements to the property refinanced, very little of the refinanced debt adds to the tax basis of the property. When the property is exchanged, the refinanced debt often shows up as taxable boot.

The only mortgage debt that counts towards basis is the "initial acquisition indebtedness" (which is part of the acquisition cost) and "property improvement indebtedness" (which goes directly into capital improvements). All other encumbrances on the property are excluded from the tax basis accounting. Equity accounting is affected, but not basis accounting.

There always has to be a basis starting point. This is "cost or other basis" at time of one's initial acquisition of the property. The term "cost" means that the property was acquired in an arm's-length purchase. The term "other basis" means that the property was acquired by other than direct purchase. It could have been acquired in a prior exchange, for example. It also could have been acquired by gift, bequest, conversion, substitution, foreclosure, and so on. However acquired, there is some finite starting basis. This *includes* all appurtenant land.

During the period of holding property, and up to the date of its disposition, there are *adjustments to basis*. The rules for adjustments to basis are set forth in **Section 1016(a)**. The general rule pertinent to real estate reads in extracted part as—

> *Proper adjustment in respect of the property shall in all cases be made—*
> *(1) . . . for expenditures, receipts, losses, or other items, properly chargeable to capital account;*
> *(2) . . . for exhaustion, wear and tear, obsolescence, amortization, and depletion,* **to the extent of the amount** *. . . allowed as deductions in computing taxable income for the taxable year or prior taxable years.* [Emphasis added.]

As you can sense from Section 1016(a), there are plus adjustments and minus adjustments to basis. We generalize them all in Figure 10.3. The message that we are trying to get across there, as well as back in Chapter 2, is that you need to keep track of all adjustments to basis, as you go along. Don't wait until after an exchange is over, when the property belongs to someone else, to try to reconstruct your tax basis. This is why we call this matter "Step 2" in your exchange planning.

For illustration purposes, consider that your initial basis (purchase price plus closing costs) of Property A in Figure 10.2 is $150,000. You refinanced the property several times, which cost

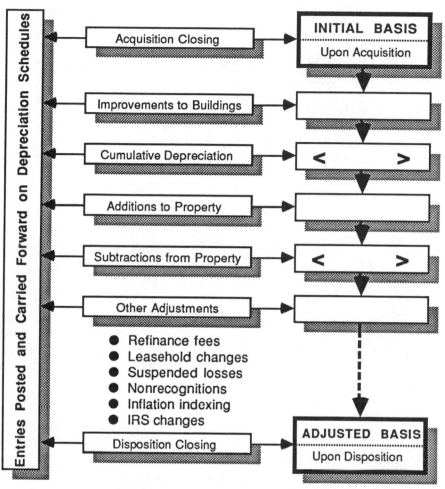

Fig. 10.3 - Adjustments to Tax Basis in Property Conveyed

you $7,000 in "points," fees, etc. You added $35,000 in capital improvements to the property. During the period of holding the rental property up to the date of conveyance in the exchange, you had cumulatively claimed $32,000 in depreciation. What is your adjusted basis in the property at the time it is conveyed (relinquished) in a Section 1031 exchange?

Using Figure 10.3 as a sequential guide, your adjusted basis would be:

$150,000 + $35,000 + <$32,000> + $7,000 = $160,000
Acq. cost   Improv.   Depr.   Refin. cost

We'll use this information later in our comprehensive example coming up in Figure 10.5.

Time Restrictions

If you want to instigate a Section 1031 exchange, you do not have unlimited time in which to do so. The exchange must be completed within a specified length of time *after* your property is relinquished. Two statutory dates are prescribed. These dates are—

(A)   45 days for the replacement property to be *identified* (the "identification period").

(B)   180 days (or due date of tax return, if earlier) for the replacement property to be *received* (the "completion period").

The statutory wording on point is subsection 1031(a)(3). The official heading of this subsection is: ***Requirement that property be identified and that exchange be completed not more than 180 days after transfer of exchanged property***.

The 180 days is the absolute limit; there are no exceptions. In some cases, the statutory time restriction is less than 180 days. This happens when the due date of the return (with allowance for extension) is less than 180 days after the property to be exchanged is relinquished. Most Form 1040 tax returns are due April 15. This means that the intended exchange activities should commence sometime before October 15.

Subsection 1031(a)(3) reads in full as follows:

*For purposes of this subsection, any property received by the taxpayer shall be treated as property which is **not like-kind** property if—*
(A)   such property is not identified as property to be received in the exchange on or before the day which is 45 days after the date on which the taxpayer transfers the property relinquished in the exchange, or
*(B)   such property is received after the **earlier** of—*

(i) the day which is 180 days after the date on which the taxpayer transfers the property relinquished in the exchange, or
(ii) the due date (determined with regard to extension) for the transferor's return of the tax imposed by this chapter for the taxable year in which the transfer of the relinquished property occurs. [Emphasis added.]

If you wish to count them, there are approximately 100 words in the above quoted subsection. The IRS has promulgated approximately 10,000 words of regulations on the time periods mentioned. These regulations are identified as Reg. 1.1031(a)-3(a) through 1.1031(a)-3(n). They espouse special rules for the identification period and for the completion period. For example, during the identification period, one is allowed to identify three alternate properties without regard to value, *or* to identify any number of alternate properties provided their aggregate value does not exceed 200% of the relinquished property value. When the 45-day identification period has passed, at least one of the properties must be accepted within the completion period. If not, the exchange fails and relinquished property is treated as a sale.

Multiple Parties in Escrow

An exchange is far more complex than an outright sale. In a sale, there is one seller and one buyer. The seller accepts from the buyer whatever money and other property is willingly offered. And that's it. The transaction is fully taxable. There is no deferment of capital gain of any kind.

Rarely in a tax-deferred exchange of like-kind properties are two parties only involved. Owner A may want Owner B's property, but it is doubtful that Owner B would want A's property (or vice versa). More likely, Owner B wants Owner C's property. Though Owner C may be willing to sell, he does not want A's property; he wants cash (or the equivalent). So, a Buyer D has to be found for A's property, who puts up the cash. Try to do *this* multiparty exchange without going through escrow!

Escrow is the legal process of holding transactions in limbo until all contractual conditions have been met.

During the escrow process, the escrow officer holds all funds, receives all properties (like and nonlike), requires professional appraisals on the properties, acknowledges new loans and debt assumptions, searches existing titles on the properties, seeks removal (or satisfaction) of encumbrances, liens, and debts, arranges for title clearances, provides for the issuance of new titles and dispenses the properties to their respective new owners at time of escrow closing.

The function of the escrow (title) company is to guarantee legal title to all properties transferred. Its function is *not* to guarantee compliance with the Section 1031 requirements. Even if the identification and completion requirements are not timely met, there are still legal titles to be perfected. Whether the transactions comprise a taxable sale or a tax-deferred exchange is not the title company's concern.

As the exchange instigator, if you want special attention to assure compliance with Section 1031, you must employ a "facilitator": a *qualified intermediary*. IRS Regulation 1.1031(k)-(1)(g)(4)(iii) defines such a person as the "taxpayer's transferee" who—

(A) Is not the taxpayer or a related party . . . and,

(B) For a fee, acts to facilitate the deferred exchange by entering into an agreement with the taxpayer for the exchange of properties pursuant to which such person acquires the relinquished property from the taxpayer (either on its own behalf or as the agent of any party to the transaction), acquires the replacement property (either on its own behalf or as the agent of any party to the transaction) and transfers the replacement property to the taxpayer.

Professional facilitators require a written contract between themselves and the instigating exchanger. They agree to do their best to comply with all published IRS regulations concerning exchanges. However, they will make no guarantee as to the tax results. They insist that the exchanger consult with his own tax advisor on the final computations for the exchange.

Basis Transfer: Step 5

In a qualified exchange, there must be tax continuity between the property relinquished and the property acquired. One's *basis transfer* is the cross-over mechanism for achieving this tax continuity. This is one of the hardest concepts to get across to property exchangers.

To exemplify, suppose one had exchangeable property worth $100,000 with a tax basis of $30,000. Assume that he acquires like property also worth $100,000. What is the exchanger's tax basis in the property acquired?

Answer: $30,000.

In a like-kind exchange, the basis in the property relinquished is transferred across-the-board directly to the property acquired. Many taxpayers tend to think that their basis in the property acquired is its exchange value: $100,000 in the example above. If the acquired property were bought for $100,000 instead of being acquired by exchange, the initial basis would be its purchase cost. But, in an exchange, one's basis in his former property is simply transferred to become the starting basis for his like-kind property received.

To the transferred basis one adds any money that he puts into the exchange, any additional debt that he assumes, and the fair market value of any nonlike property that he contributes to make the deal go through. This concept of basis accounting in the property acquired is depicted diagrammatically in Figure 10.4.

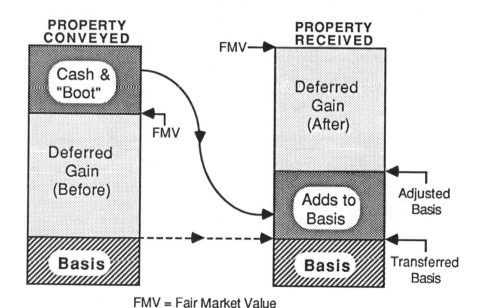

FMV = Fair Market Value

Fig. 10.4 - The Concept of "Basis Transfer" Upon Exchange

The assumption in Figure 10.4 is that the property acquired is higher in value than the property relinquished. Cash and boot have to be paid. This is the simple form of of exchange: an up-exchange. In a down-exchange, cash and boot are received, at least a portion of which is taxable. It is the taxable portion of the cash and boot only that adds to the transferred basis.

The role of basis transfer is stated more fully — and more cloudily — in Section 1031(d): *Basis*. We hesitate to cite this section to you in full. We propose, instead, to cite highlights from this section, then give you a comprehensive example below, to illustrate how the basis-new computations work.

Accordingly, Section 1031(d) reads in selected part as follows:

> *If property was acquired on an exchange described in this section, . . . then the basis **shall be the same** as that of the property exchanged, **decreased** in the amount of any money received . . . and **increased in the amount of gain** or decreased in the amount of loss . . . **recognized on such exchange**. If the property so acquired consisted in part of . . . other property, the basis . . . shall be allocated between the properties (other than money) received. . . . Where as part of the consideration to the taxpayer another party to the exchange assumed a liability of the taxpayer or acquired from the taxpayer property subject to a liability, **such assumption or acquisition** (in the amount of the liability) **shall be considered as money received** by the taxpayer on the exchange. [Emphasis added.]*

The last sentence immediately above makes it quite clear that debt relief and debt assumption are a valid form of money (consideration). Debt relief is treated as cash received, whereas debt assumption is treated as cash paid. Real estate exchanges are characterized by "debt swapping," as such properties almost invariably include mortgage indebtedness of one kind or another.

Comprehensive Example

When the real estate brokers (and their attorneys), title companies (and their attorneys), exchange facilitators (and their attorneys) are all through — and you have paid their commissions and fees — you still have a major task ahead. There is the preparation of a comprehensive summary of the exchange process so as to be ready for the IRS. It is for this reason that a comprehensive example of the tax accounting procedures is necessary.

In preparing your summary for the IRS, it is helpful to keep the following major steps in mind:

Step 1 — Equity Balance: Boot
Step 2 — Basis of Property Conveyed
Step 3 — Gain Realized on Exchange
Step 4 — Taxable Gain; Deferred Gain
Step 5 — Basis Transfer & Reallocation

With these steps in mind, let us assume a down-exchange (that is, the acquired property is less in value than the property conveyed). We will also assume that two like-kind properties are acquired for one property give up. This necessitates that the transfer of old basis to the two acquired properties be allocated. Let us assume that all three properties are residential rental real estate. This is the most common form of Section 1031 exchanges.

The situation is this. You instigate the exchange and convey Property A worth $365,000. You identify and timely acquire Property B (worth $130,000) and, separately, Property C (worth $170,000). You have a mortgage debt on Property A of $285,000 which the "buyer" (who is *not* Owner B or C) agrees to assume. In turn, you agree to assume the Property B mortgage of $100,000 and the Property C mortgage of $150,000. You also agree to pay all of the exchange expenses which amount to $35,000 (including the standard sales commission on Property A). You receive $30,000 in "boot" of which $10,000 is cash and $20,000 is other property (furniture and appliances) associated with Property C (as per Figure 10.2). Your adjusted basis in Property A is $160,000 (as per Figure 10.3 and its accompanying text).

What is your capital gain realized on the exchange? How much of this gain, if any, is tax recognized? How much of the gain is tax deferred? What is your transfer basis in Property B? What is your transfer basis in Property C?

We present all of the sequential computations in Figure 10.5. We urge you to read through Figure 10.5 rather slowly. It illustrates why an exchange computation cannot be done off the top of one's head or on the back of an envelope. It also illustrates why exchanges are undertaken when there is substantial capital gain.

Taxpayer Relinquishes Property A (with Tax Basis Of $160,000) and Acquires Two Properties: B and C. The Existing Mortgage Debts are Swapped.

Step 1: Equity Balance: Boot
See Fig. 10.2 | FMV = Fair Market Value |

Boot Received

(a) Cash (money)	$10,000	
(b) Boot (noncash) FMV	20,000	
		30,000

Step 2: Basis of Property Conveyed
See Fig. 10.3 (and accompanying text)

Adjusted Basis

(a) Property A	$160,000	
		160,000

Step 3: Gain Realized

Consideration Received

(a) Property B (FMV)	$130,000	
(b) Property C (FMV)	170,000	
(c) Cash (money)	10,000	
(d) Boot (noncash) FMV	20,000	
(e) Debt relief (A)	285,000	
		615,000

Consideration Paid

(a) Property A (basis)	$160,000	
(b) Debt assumed (B)	100,000	
(c) Debt assumed (C)	150,000	
(d) Exchange expenses	35,000	
		< 445,000 >

GAIN REALIZED ON EXCHANGE: $170,000   [I]

Step 4: Taxable Gain; Deferred Gain

Cash and Boot Received

(a) Actual Cash	$10,000	
(b) Boot (noncash)	20,000	
(c) Debt relief (A)	285,000	
		315,000

(Continued on next page)

Fig. 10.5 - Comprehensive Example of Like-Kind Exchange

Step 4: (Continued from previous page)

Cash & Boot Paid

(a) Debt assumed (B)	$100,000	
(b) Debt assumed (C)	150,000	
(c) Exchange expenses	35,000	
		<285,000>

NET CASH & BOOT RECEIVED: $30,000 **[II]**

Taxable Gain = Lower of I or II = 30,000
Deferred Gain = I Minus II = 140,000
170,000

Step 5: Basis Transfer & Reallocation

(a) Initial basis transfer 160,000
(b) The PLUS adjustments

● Taxable gain	$30,000	
● Exchange expenses	35,000	
● Debt assumed (B)	100,000	
● Debt assumed (C)	150,000	
		315,000

(c) The MINUS adjustments

● Cash received	$10,000	
● Boot received	20,000	
● Debt relieved (A)	285,000	
		<315,000>

STARTING BASIS IN B & C: $160,000

(d) Allocation of Basis

Basis in B = 160,000 x 43.33% =	69,328
Basis in C = 160,000 x 56.67% =	90,672
	$160,000

FMV Property B	=	$130,000	= 43.33%
FMV Property C	=	170,000	= 56.67%
		300,000	100.00%

Fig. 10.5 - Comprehensive Example of Like-Kind Exchange

As Step 3 in Figure 10.5 illustrates, the amount of capital gain realized in the exchange transaction has to be expressly determined (whether taxed or not). The amount of gain illustrated is $170,000. Of this amount, $30,000 is taxed now and $140,000 is tax deferred. The $30,000 taxed is the total boot received (cash and noncash). The $140,000 of gain which is deferred actually finds its way into the replacement properties as a rollover adjustment (reduction) in the FMV's of properties B and C. Let's check this out:

$$\text{FMV of A + B} = \$130,000 + \$170,000 \quad = \quad \$300,000$$
$$\text{Deferred gain "rolled over"} \qquad\qquad = \quad <\!140,\!000\!>$$
$$\text{Difference} \quad = \quad \$160,000$$

Isn't this $160,000 the adjusted basis of Property A conveyed? We traded down (*received* cash & boot) rather than trading up (cash & boot conveyed) as portrayed in Figure 10.4.

When Properties B and C are subsequently sold, the aggregate deferred gain "pops out of the computations" in taxable form.

Must Use Form 8824

Having taken you (rather painstakingly) through the computational features of an exchange, where do you report the Figure 10.5-type information on your tax return?

Answer: This is where IRS Form 8824:: **Like-Kind Exchanges**, comes in. You must use it. A subheading on this form says—

Attach to your tax return. Use a separate form for each like-kind exchange.

Form 8824 is designed to accommodate all kinds of Section 1031 exchanges, in addition to rental real estate. As such, the official form tends to be hodgepodgey and confusing. Much of its focus is on related party transactions, conflict-of-interest sales, and nonlike property that you may have given as boot. The gutsy issues of the like-kind properties are relegated to only a few lines. For example, the total consideration received is entered on two lines; the total consideration paid is entered on one line. The difference between these two totals is the realized gain or loss on the exchange.

The realized gain or loss is the maximum capital gain or capital loss that would be tax recognized if the transaction were a sale, and not an exchange. As such, the realized amount is a very critical computation which requires more than just a few lines on an official form. This is why we went to the length that we did in Figure 10.5.

From the realized gain or loss, the recognized gain (that which is taxable) emerges, as do the tax-deferred gain and the starting basis of the property (or properties) received. Each of these four conclusionary elements of the exchange appears on one separate line on Form 8824. This is a skimpy way of treating a matter with such potentially high tax stakes. Generally, rental real estate exchanges involve entry line figures of several hundreds of thousands of dollars, or more.

Nevertheless, with the foregoing in mind, we present in Figure 10.6 an abbreviated, edited, and *revised* version of Form 8824. We have purposely omitted all entry spaces for related party and conflict-of-interest transactions (as being too distractive). For simplicity, we also have omitted lines for nonlike property that you may have conveyed. When you *convey* nonlike property, your gain or loss on that property is computed as a separate transaction on its own. It is not treated as part of the exchange, as is the case when you *receive* nonlike property.

Caution: The line numbers in Figure 10.6, though consecutive with those on the official form, differ substantially from the official line numbers. When you look at the official form, you'll know instantly why we have done this.

With reference to Figure 10.6, there are two particular entries to which we want to call your attention. These are lines 2 (*net* liabilities assumed by other party) and 7 (*net* liabilities assumed by you). Only one line or the other will apply: not both in the same exchange. These lines represent the "debt swapping" of mortgages that takes place between rental property exchangers. Line 2 is debt relief to you and is treated as money received. Line 7 is additional debt assumed by you and is treated as a basis addition to the like-kind property (or properties) received.

Realty Reportings: 1099-S

You go through all of the exchange computations that we illustrate in Figure 10.5 and sequentially summarize in Figure 10.6. What does the IRS's computer "see"?

Form 8824	LIKE-KIND EXCHANGES		Year
Your Name		Your Soc. Sec. No.	

Description and Dates of Like-Kind

Property Conveyed	Property Received
● Date acquired	● Date identified
● Date conveyed	● Date received

Omitted Matters (See Text)

1	Cash and FMV of nonlikes received		
2	Net liabilities assumed by other party		
3	FMV of like-property received		
4	**Total Consideration Received**		
5	Adjusted basis of like-property conveyed		
6	Cash and FMV of nonlikes paid		
7	Net liabilities assumed by you		
8	Exchange expenses you paid		
9	**Total Consideration Conveyed**		
10	REALIZED GAIN OR <LOSS>: Subtract line 9 from line 4		
11	RECOGNIZED GAIN : Enter SMALLER of lines 1 plus 2, or 10 ▶ BUT NOT LESS THAN ZERO		
12	DEFERRED GAIN OR <LOSS>: Subtract line 11 from line 10		
13	Transfer of basis: Add lines 9 and 11		
14	Adjustment to basis: Add lines 1 and 2		
15	STARTING BASIS OF LIKE PROPERTY RECEIVED ▶ Subtract line 14 from line 13		

Fig. 10.6 - Abbreviated, Edited, and Revised Version of Form 8824

It sees three separate Forms 1099-S, each reporting the gross proceeds (FMV) for properties A, B, and C. It does not know — and does not care — that Property A was exchanged for Properties B and C. Separately, there'll be a 1099-S(A) showing $365,000; a 1099-S(B) showing $130,000; and a 1099-S(C) showing $170,000. Each Form 1099 will describe each property briefly, show its closing date (when title transfers), and indicate any boot (other than cash) to be received by the transferor. In our example case in Figure 10.5 the transferor is property owner A.

Who prepares and submits to the IRS the 1099-S information returns?

Answer: Any "real estate reporting person."

Such a person is defined in Code Section 6045(e)(2) as—

Any of the following persons involved in a real estate transaction in the following order:
  (A) the person (including any attorney or title company) responsible for closing the transaction,
  (B) the mortgage lender,
  (C) the seller's broker,
  (D) the buyer's broker, or
  (E) such other person who (for a consideration) acts as a middleman with respect to property or services.

The official title of Form 1099-S is: **Statement for Recipients of Proceeds from Real Estate Transactions.** This form is required for the reporting of all realty sales and exchanges, whether the property is residential, commercial, industrial, farmland, or unimproved land. Whether the transaction is a tax-deferred exchange or not, it is IRS computer-treated as a full-blown *sale . . . with zero tax basis.* This puts all the onus on you — the transferor/exchanger — to do your homework and report it properly on your Form 1040.

Where on Form 1040?

The IRS expects you to show somewhere on your Form 1040 an entry that exact-matches the Form 1099-S gross proceeds reported to it following any realty exchange. As previously described, you are instructed to report each like-kind exchange on Form 8824. Unfortunately, there is no entry box on Form 8824 which says (in effect): "Show gross proceeds from this exchange reported on Form 1099-S." Had there been such a box, we would have certainly highlighted it in Figure 10.6.

Fortunately, the general instructions to Form 8824, citing its purpose, are helpful. These instructions say—

Form 8824 is used as a supporting statement for like-kind exchanges reported on other forms including Form 4797:

Sales of Business Property, and the **Schedule D** *(1040): Capital Gains and Losses, for your tax return. See the instructions for Form 4797 or Schedule D for how to report the exchange on those forms.*

Of the two referenced forms (4797 and Sch. D), the one on which you can clearly isolate and reconcile with the Form(s) 1099-S is Form 4797. Line 1 thereon reads:

Enter here the gross proceeds from the sale or exchange of real estate reported to you on Form(s) 1099-S (or a substitute statement).

This is your cue that the IRS's computer will be looking at your return and comparing it with what the real estate reporting person reports.

The instructions to Form 4797 (subheaded: Exchange of "Like-Kind" Property) tells you to—

Report on Form 4797 the exchange of like-kind property, even if no gain or loss is recognized. Write "From Form 8824" for the description of the property, and enter the gain from Form 8824, if any. Also, write in the top margin of Form 4797 "Like-Kind Exchange."

In other words, the **recognized gain** from Form 8824, if any (line 11 in Figure 10.6), winds up on Form 4797. There, it combines with gains and losses from other business property capital transactions. The net gain, if any, on Form 4797 winds up on Schedule D (1040) at the line which reads: *Gain from Form 4797.* Once on Schedule D, the exchange gain combines with other capital gains and losses, having nothing to do with the realty exchange process.

11

INSTALLMENT SALES

Property Sales With Large Capital Gains Are "Naturals" For Installment Method Taxing (Via Form 6252). Essential To The Process Is An Installment Obligation With All Payment Terms Specified. "Payments Received" Includes ALL FORMS OF CONSIDERATION Constituting The Selling Price. The Taxable Portion Of Each Payment Is Based On A Gross Profit Ratio (GPR) Which Remains Fixed Year After Year. The Balance Due On The CONTRACT PRICE Is The "Tracking Target" For Installment Satisfaction. Special Rules Apply To Income Recapture, Pledges Of Installment Obligations, And Dispositions Before Maturity.

Another form of deferred tax treatment is the installment method of sale. Whereas a like-kind exchange is the deferment of gain to be taxed, an installment sale defers the payments on gain. That is, the gain is determined at time of sale, but the payment of tax thereon is spread over the duration of installments paid to the seller by the buyer. Thus, technically, installment sales are *deferred payment* sales: not deferred gain sales.

An installment sale is an outright sale. Full legal title passes to the buyer. Other than cash, boot (noncash), debt assumption(s), and installment obligation(s), there is no exchange of like-properties involved. There is no involuntary conversion; there is no "other disposition" (such as into a trust). It is a pure sale which is fully tax accountable in the year of sale.

Another characteristic of installment taxing is its application to gains only: not to losses. After all, on a loss there is no gain to be taxed. This is so whether the sale price is paid immediately . . . or stretched out over many years. Installment losses are treated as a one-time loss, no different from other business loss situations.

In this chapter, we want to present the tax accounting features of installment gain, and touch on some of the terms and restrictions that apply. In doing so, we want to remind you that our focus is on individual owners (and co-owners) of rental realty: *not* dealers in property. We will also sidestep related-party transactions because of the very special rules that apply. (We will, however, touch on related-party transactions in the next chapter.)

Installment Prerequisites

The culmination of a tax-qualified installment sale is an enforceable legal obligation by the buyer to the seller. That is, full title (in fee simple) passes to the buyer, subject only to some form of *installment obligation* by the buyer. The obligation must be in writing and be enforceable under state and local law. Enforceability implies that the obligation must be secured by a *deed of trust* against the property sold. These are everyday, ordinary features of an installment sale consummated through a licensed real estate broker.

Hence, the first (tax) prerequisite is a legal installment note under state and local law.

The second prerequisite is that the face amount (initial obligation) of the note be stated in U.S. dollars only. The value of any other property or services that may have been included in the selling price, and remain unpaid, should *not* be included in the installment dollar amount. Said amount should be prominently displayed in the upper left-hand corner of the note, together with its date and place of execution. This is called the "face value" of the note, because of its prominence of display. The indicated amount is the initial *principal* only.

A third prerequisite is that the rate of interest on the amount of principal due be clearly stated on the face of the note. The rate should be a fixed percentage per annum. A variable rate should not be used unless it is keyed to commonly accepted government obligations, such as U.S. Treasury Notes. The intended payment dates should be clearly designated for properly determining when the interest is due. In all cases, the rate of interest should be at competitive market rates, at the time the note is executed.

Installment sellers of real estate are particularly cautioned to avoid unstated, or below-market interest rates. Low-interest or no-interest installment notes are always tax suspect. The suspicion is that one has intentionally buried interest in with the principal, in order to avoid ordinary tax on it. Unless the rate of interest is stated clearly and competitively, harsh imputed-interest penalty rules come into play (namely, Sections 483 and 1274).

There is a fourth prerequisite. As you know, installment payments typically include principal *and* interest, simultaneously. You MUST SEPARATE these two items. The principal is subject to installment gain computations, whereas the interest is not. For this separation, you are well advised to accompany each installment note with an "amortization table" showing the payment due dates, and the separation of principal and interest on each of those dates.

And, finally, there is a fifth tax prerequisite. There must be a specific *maturity date* for each note. The payoff may be "on or before" such date. A clear or determinable end-of-the-line due date must be indicated. Otherwise, the installment payments could go on indefinitely. The indefinite stretch-out and deferment of tax is not the intent of the installment sale rules.

In way of summarizing the above prerequisites, we present Figure 11.1. It is our version of an installment note for tax-reporting purposes only. You are cautioned not to use it other than as an illustrative sample. Your realty broker will have a preprinted form which is legal in your area.

Code Section 453

Installment sales are most beneficial when there is large capital gain, and when the gross sale price is substantial. By "substantial," we mean a selling price which is $100,000 or more. This dollar magnitude is readily associated with rental real estate, whether it be a single family residence, a multi-unit complex, or a sharecropping farm. These assets are potentially large gainers. The whole theory of installment taxing is that one should not be taxed on his capital gain until he actually receives it.

The basic rules on installment taxing of capital gain are embodied in Section 453 of the IR Code. Its official heading is: *Installment Method*. It consists of 12 subsections comprising approximately 2,800 words.

As with most tax laws, Section 453 is lengthy and covers some entirely different situations from those under discussion here. The

```
╔═══════════════════════════════════════════════════╗
║              INSTALLMENT  NOTE                       ║
║                                                      ║
║   $    (amount)          (place)           (date)    ║
║   ─────────────    ──────────────    ─────────────   ║
║                                                      ║
║   In installments as herein stated, I promise to pay to   (seller)    ║
║   at ____(place)____ the sum of ____(amount)____ DOLLARS with ║
║   interest from _____(date)_____ on unpaid principal at the rate of ║
║   _____ per cent per annum; principal and interest payable ║
║   in installments of __(amount)__ Dollars on the _____ day ║
║   of each month,  beginning on the _____ day of (month/year) ║
║   and continuing until said principal and interest have been paid on ║
║   or before ___(final date)___ .                     ║
║                                                      ║
║   Should default be made in payment of any installment of principal ║
║   or interest when due, the whole sum of principal and interest shall ║
║   become immediately due at the option of the holder of this note. ║
║   This note is secured by a DEED OF TRUST.           ║
║                                                      ║
║     /s/                          /s/                 ║
║   ─────────────────        ─────────────────────     ║
║       BUYER (H)                  BUYER (W)           ║
╚═══════════════════════════════════════════════════╝
```

Fig. 11.1 - Sample of an Installment Sale Obligation

general rules are succinct, and are espoused in subsections (a), (b), and (c). Subsections (d) through (l) cover special situations, such as related-taxpayer transactions, marketable indebtedness, sales to a controlled entity, certain corporate liquidations, dealer dispositions, revolving credit plans, election out, and recognition of recapture income.

The tax code headings to subsections 453(a) through (c) are:

(a) *General rule*
(b) *Installment sale defined*
(c) *Installment method defined*

Subsec. (a) is just one sentence. It reads—

Except as otherwise provided in this section, income from an installment sale shall be taken into account for purposes of . . . the installment method.

The phrase "except as otherwise provided," refers to subsections (d) through (j).

Subsections (b) and (c) read in pertinent part as follows:

(b)   The term "installment sale" means a disposition of property where at least 1 payment is to be received after the close of the taxable year in which the disposition occurs. . . . The term . . . does not include . . . any dealer disposition.

*(c)   The term "installment method" means a method under which the income recognized for any taxable year from a disposition is that proportion of the payments received in that year which the **gross profit** (realized or to be realized when payment is completed) bears to the **total contract price**.* [Emphasis added.]

As you'll see shortly, the key to understanding installment sale capital gain, year after year, is the gross profit percentage computed at time of sale. This means that we'll come back to subsection 453(c) in the computational mechanics.

Introduction to Form 6252

The computational aspects of installment taxing are set forth step-by-step on IRS Form 6252. Many of its line entries have quite satisfactory explanations on the face of the form itself. Its official heading is: **Installment Sale Income.** Just below this heading is an instruction which reads—

See separate instructions.   Attach to your tax return. Use separate form for each sale or other disposition of property on the installment method.

Thus, immediately, if you have more than one installment sale outstanding, you need to sequentially number the forms in the order of the sale dates.

Form 6252 is quite straightforward as tax forms go. In fact, it can be highly useful to a conscientious seller who wants to keep track of his installment receipts and match them cumulatively with his gain being taxed. The form is used each year in which an installment payment is received. Consequently, we think it is essential that you be familiar with its general format and contents.

With no attempt to duplicate the official Form 6252 (you know it will change by the time you read this), we present a generalized version of it in Figure 11.2. Note that it consists of three parts, namely:

Part I   — **Gross Profit and Contract Price**
                 (complete for year of sale only)
Part II   — **Installment Sale Income**
                 (complete for any year payment received)
Part III   — **Related Party Installment Sale**
                 (complete for sale year and 2 years thereafter)

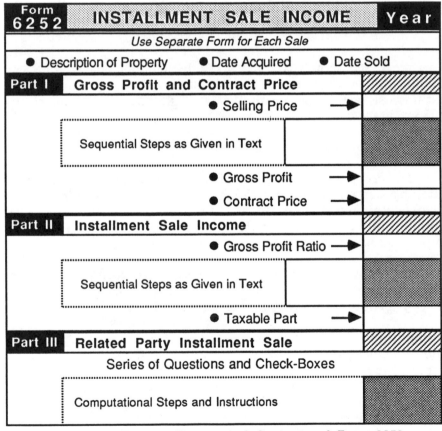

Fig. 11.2 - General Format and Contents of Form 6252

Because of the importance of understanding installment tax accounting, we will take you through the primary portions of Parts I and II. We will omit any discussion of Part III in this chapter.

The general instructions to Form 6252 tell you to—

Use Form 6252 to report income from **casual** *sales of real property . . . if you will receive* **any payments** *in the tax year* **after** *the year of sale. If any part of an installment payment you received is for interest,* **be sure** *to report that interest on the appropriate . . . schedule.* [Emphasis added.]

This instruction is telling you several things. First, the form is for *casual* sales of real estate only. This eliminates its applicability to dealer sales. Secondly, the form is to be used when *any payment* is received after the year of sale. This includes principal-only receipts, interest-only receipts, principal-interest combinations, and *any other* consideration received. And, thirdly, the instruction is telling you to *be sure* to separate principal and interest, and to report the interest "elsewhere" on your return.

Form 6252 is for **payments on principal** only. These payments include two types of tax-accountable money. Part of each payment is return of capital (which is *not* taxed); part is capital gain (which is taxed). Hence, the underlying and primary purpose of Form 6252 is to separate the taxable from the nontaxable portions of the payments on principal. To do this properly, you need to know your gross profit from each sale.

Computation of Gross Profit

The gross profit on an installment sale is computed the same way as if the sale were all cash: without installments. The idea is to know what the gross profit *eventually* will be, when all payments on principal have been made. For this eventuality, there are two computational sequences: short and long. The short sequence is helpful for grasping the key concepts involved.

The short sequence to gross profit (and return of capital) is:

1. Gross sale price (the contracted selling price agreed to between seller and buyer)
2. Adjusted basis in property sold
3. Commissions and other expenses of sale
4. Add steps 2 and 3

5. Subtract step 4 from step 1
   = **Gross Profit** (*taxable part*)
6. Subtract step 5 from step 1
   = **Return of Capital** (*nontaxable part*)

This sequence is overly simplified, particularly for rental real estate involving mortgage assumptions, wrap-arounds, contingent sales, and "income recapture."

The proper computational sequence is a 10-step process, line by line, as it appears officially on Form 6252. These 10 official steps are:

Step 1 — Selling price (*including the down payment, assumed mortgages, other debts assumed, the installment note, and any other property at FMV received*).

Step 2 — Mortgages and other debts buyer assumed (*strictly those existing on the property at time of sale; exclude the installment note or any new mortgages the buyer gets*).

Step 3 — Subtract Step 2 from Step 1.

Step 4 — Cost or other basis of property sold.

Step 5 — Depreciation allowed or allowable.

Step 6 — Adjusted basis. Subtract Step 5 from Step 4.

Step 7 — Commissions and other expenses of sale.

Step 8 — Income recapture from Form 4797, Part III.

Step 9 — *Installment sale basis.* Add Steps 6, 7, and 8.

Step 10 — Subtract Step 9 from Step 1.
   = **Gross Profit**

Mortgages and Other Debts

Steps 1 and 2 in the official sequence above are a little tricky and can lead (unintentionally) to a higher gross profit, or to a lower gross profit, than is proper. We tried to forewarn you of this by including italicized instructions to each of these steps.

In the real world, rental property is often mortgaged to the hilt. Some property owners like to keep their equity to a minimum by borrowing against it or refinancing at every opportunity. The result can be a hodgepodge of mortgage-type debt distinguished as qualified, nonqualified, and wrap-around debt.

Qualified debt is that which is incurred in order to acquire, hold, or operate the property. Most of this debt is secured by the property itself and is a legitimate part of the "cost or other basis" of the property (at Step 4 above).

Nonqualified debt is that which is unrelated to acquiring, holding, or operating the property. It is a form of "draw down" of equity that is used for other projects or personal expenditures of the owner. Said debt may or may not be secured by the property. If unsecured, it becomes a creditor's lien against the property at time of sale. Nonqualified debt is *not* part of the property's "cost or other basis." If assumed by the buyer, it becomes part of the payment received in year of sale. It is subtracted (at Step 3) from the selling price, to subsequently affect the "contract price."

Wrap-around debt is an arrangement whereby the buyer does not assume directly any of the mortgage-type debt on the property. Instead, an entirely new installment note is prepared which "wraps" the old debt with entirely new debt. The seller remains obligated to pay off the old debt; the buyer is obligated only to the seller for the wrap-around note. Since the buyer neither assumes nor takes the property subject to the wrapped indebtedness, the wrapped debt is not subtracted from the selling price for determining the contract price. In other words, the wrap-around note, since it is new, is *not* included in Step 2. Therefore, it does not affect Step 3. As we'll see, Step 3 directly influences the contract price.

"Contract Price" Explained

In order to determine the taxable portion of each installment payment, we need to explain the term "contract price." It is not the same as selling price, though in some cases it might be. Much depends on the existing debt on the property and what portion of that debt is assumed by the buyer.

The contract price is composed of *two* components. One component is the total amount of cash ultimately payable to the seller. If the property is sold with qualifying (cost or other basis) debt on it, and the buyer assumes all of that debt (or takes the property subject to such debt), the seller obviously will receive less cash than that which is represented by the selling price. Therefore, the installment contract price will differ from the gross sale price. If the buyer did not assume any of the seller's debt whatsoever, only then would the sale price and contract price be the same.

The second component of contract price is what is called: *excess debt over basis*. This occurs when nonqualifying debt (equity draw-downs and personal debt encumbrances) is added to the qualifying debt, whereupon the total exceeds the installment sale basis in the property. When this happens, and the buyer assumes this excess debt, the contract price will be greater than the selling price less qualified debt.

Let us illustrate the difference between contract price and selling price with a simple numerical example.

Property having a basis of $80,000 is sold for $70,000 cash subject to an existing mortgage of $60,000. Here, the term "cash" includes the installment note. The selling price is $130,000 (70,000 cash plus 60,000 mortgage assumed). The contract price, however, is $70,000 (130,000 *less* the 60,000 debt assumed by the buyer).

In this example, if the basis were $40,000 instead of $80,000 (with the same $60,000 mortgage), there would be "excess debt over basis." The amount of this excess debt would be $20,000 (60,000 mortgage less 40,000 basis). In this case, the contract price would be $90,000 (70,000 cash plus 20,000 debt-over-basis). Debt-over-basis, when assumed by the buyer, is treated as additional cash money received by the seller. Thus, the contract price becomes higher than the actual installment payments to be received, because the seller used the debt-over-basis money without previously paying tax on it. His debt habits are now catching up with him. He pays tax on his excess debt in year of sale.

Gross Profit "Ratio"

The next order of business is to determine the seller's Gross Profit Ratio . . . **GPR**, as it is called. This is the ratio of the expected gross profit to the total contract price. Once determined, this ratio remains fixed throughout the installment period. This is the substance of subsection 453(c), quoted in full earlier.

For determining this ratio, let us continue with the step sequence above. Step 10, recall, is the gross profit. As a reminder, gross profit is the gross selling price (Step 1) *less* the installment sale basis (Step 9) in the property.

Steps 11 through 14 now become:

Step 11 — Step 3 revisited (*selling price less all debt on the property assumed by the buyer*).
= Net cash to seller.

Step 12 — Subtract Step 9 (*installment sale basis*) from Step 2 (*mortgages and other debts the buyer assumed or took the property subject to*).

= Excess debt over basis, if any. If zero or less, enter zero.

Step 13 — **Contract price.** Add Steps 11 and 12.

Step 14 — **Gross profit ratio.** Divide Step 10 by Step 13.

$$= \frac{\text{Gross Profit}}{\text{Contract Price}} = \textbf{GPR}$$

We want to caution you that Steps 11 through 14 differ from those officially on Form 6252. Steps 1 through 10, however, are identical to the corresponding line sequence on the official form. Line 15 on Form 6252 (which corresponds to our Step 14) uses the term: Gross profit *percentage*. It does not use: Gross profit "ratio" as we have done. Mathematically, the two terms are identical. For example, if the gross profit percentage were 63.84%, the GPR would be 0.6384. A 4-decimal accuracy is usually sought in these calculations. We prefer GPR because of its simplicity in application year after year. It is preferable to write a fraction on a tax form, since the percentage symbol could be misconstrued as dollars.

Once determined, the GPR is a fixed fraction throughout the life of the installment obligation. It is used to determine the taxable part of capital gain in each installment payment. It is not uncommon for the same GPR fraction to be used for as many as 20 years.

Taxable Part of Installments

In the year of sale, there are three components which are capital gain taxed, and to which the GPR applies. These components are:

(a) excess debt over basis (Step 12 above)
(b) down payment on the sale (includes all forms of consideration received by seller)
(c) payment(s) on installment principal

The down payment is the amount of cash and boot (at fair market value) which the buyer advances, and debts of the seller assumed by the buyer, in order to consummate the sale. This information can be obtained from the escrow settlement statement.

Seldom does the seller actually receive in his pocket the full down payment shown on the settlement statement. This money is generally used to pay sales commissions, selling expenses, payoff of non-mortgage debts, and title closing costs. Nevertheless, the down payment is part of the selling price. It contains a portion of capital gains represented by the GPR.

The installment obligation arising out of the transaction is also identified on the escrow settlement statement. In addition, it is formulated as a separate document of its own. As previously illustrated (Figure 11.1), this document sets forth the face amount of principal, the annual rate of interest, the duration of installments, and other terms for payments. For the year of sale, seldom is any significant amount of principal paid on the installment obligation.

Altogether, an aggregate amount known as *payments received in year of sale* is established. Once this is done, the taxable portion of capital gain becomes a multi-step procedure.

This (official) procedure follows:

Step 15 — Gross profit percentage. (Enter 4-decimal fraction.)

Step 16 — **For year of sale only** — enter amount, if any, from Step 12 (excess debt over basis).

Step 17 — Payments received during year. (**Do not include interest whether stated or unstated.**)

Step 18 — Add Steps 16 and 17.

Step 19 — Payments received in prior years.

Step 20 — **Installment sale income.** Multiply Step 18 by Step 15.

Step 21 — Part of Step 20 that is ordinary income under recapture rules. See instructions. Enter on **Form 4797** (Sales of Business Property) at line identified as: *Ordinary gain from Form 6252.*

Step 22 — Subtract Step 21 from Step 20. Enter here and on **Schedule D** (Capital Gains and Losses) at line identified as: *Short-term (or Long-term) gain from Form 6252.*

As you can see from this sequence, the installment sale income (Step 20) goes onto two other tax forms before making its way onto your yearly summary Form 1040.

Keeping Track of Payments

Every year that you receive an installment payment — principal, interest, or other consideration — you must file Form 6252. You fill in the description of the property and date of sale at the top of the form, and then use Part II (only) thereof. The official instruction to Part II says—

> Complete this part for . . . any year you receive a payment or have certain debts you must treat as payment on installment obligations.

Under the "pledge rule" (Sec. 453A(d)), certain arrangements are *deemed* installment payments whether they are actually so or not.

The first entry line on Part II is Step 15 above. This is your gross profit percentage — your GPR. The second line entry, Step 16, is zero, as it applies only to the year of sale. You must be sure to actually enter zero, otherwise you foul up the IRS's computer which is tracking your contract price. In Figure 11.3, we show you how to enter a zero at Step 16. We also include Steps 15 through 22. These correspond with the official sequence on Form 6252.

In Figure 11.3, we particularly call your attention to Step 19: *Payments received in prior years*. Note that this step is an "aside item." It does not enter the computational part in Step 20 (nor 21, nor 22). Why, then, do you think the Step 19 entry is there?

Answer: It's all part of the computer sophistication of the IRS tracking your financial affairs.

What doesn't show up in Part II is that the **contract price** is the IRS's tracking target. Each year, its computer adds to your cumulative prior-year payments your current-year payments, and subtracts the payment totals from your contract price. The "balance due" is the amount of contract principal on which tax remains to be paid. Should, some year, a Form 6252 not show up on your tax return, the computer "searches for" any remaining balance. Should there be any unreported balance on your installment account, you'll get a computer demand for the unpaid tax . . . plus penalties . . . plus interest.

Our point is that you are well advised to do your own payment tracking, year after year. To assist you in this regard, we have intentionally added two entries in Figure 11.3 which do not appear officially on Form 6252 (Part II). One entry — Contract Price — is inserted in the white space *above* the entry line at Step 19. The

Form 6252	INSTALLMENT SALE INCOME	Year
	● Description of Property ● Date Acquired ● Date Sold	

Part II	Year(s) SUBSEQUENT to Year of Sale	
15	Gross Profit Ratio (same as year of sale)	
16	/////////////////////	- 0 -
17	Payment(s) received during year	
18	Step 17 repeated	
	▶ Contract Price	
19	Payments received prior years	
	▶ Balance Due	
20	Taxable portion of installment Step 18 x Step 15	
21	Ordinary income portion Form 4797	
22	Capital gain portion Schedule D	

Fig. 11.3 - Edited Part II of Form 6252 for "Subsequent Year(s)"

second entry — Balance Due — is inserted in the white space *below* the entry line at Step 19. Though you are not required to do so, we urge you to make these entries, in your own hand-printing, on each year's Form 6252. When the balance due on the contract price reduces to zero, Form 6252 is no longer needed.

For tax tracking, the total contract price is a fixed "given," year after year. The balance due on it is that which follows from certain subtractions, namely:

- Down payment (year of sale)
- FMV other property received
- Excess debt over basis
- Prior principal on installment note
- Current principal on installment note
- Prior pledges of installment note
- Current pledges of installment note

As you can reason from this listing of payment types, the face amount and payment terms of the installment note serve no tax tracking purpose on Form 6252. Therefore, payments on your installment note should be kept as a separate tracking document on its own. It is up to you to collect your money from the obligor.

Premature Dispositions

Figure 11.3 assumes that the installment obligation — eventually — is paid in full to the original seller of the property. Situations can arise, however, when this is not the case. The holder of the obligation may dispose of it prior to its maturity. Pledging it as security or collateral is not a disposition, unless surrendered.

An installment note may be sold (at a discount), exchanged for some other note (of similar indebtedness), endorsed as payment for major purchases, or used as boot in other capital transactions. In some cases, the note may become unenforceable or uncollectible. In these situations, the disposition of an installment note is treated as a capital asset of its own. The gain or loss thereon is tax recognized.

The tax law on point is Section 453B: *Gain or Loss on Disposition of Installment Obligations*. The general rule — Section 453B(a) — reads in part as follows:

If an installment obligation is satisfied at other than its face value or distributed, transmitted, sold, or otherwise disposed of, gain or loss shall result to the extent of the difference between the **basis of the obligation** *and—*
    (1) the amount realized, in the case of satisfaction at other than face value or a sale or exchange, **or**
    (2) the fair market value of the obligation at the time of distribution, transmission, or disposition . . . [if] otherwise than by sale or exchange.
Any gain or loss so resulting shall be considered as resulting from the sale or exchange of the property in respect of which the installment obligation was received. [Emphasis added.]

The key to understanding the above is the emphasized phrase: "basis of the obligation." This basis is defined in subsection 453B(b) as—

The excess of the face value of the obligation over an amount equal to the income which would be returnable were the obligation satisfied in full.

We need an example to illustrate this basis determination. Suppose you held an installment note with a face value of $100,000. It was paid down to $85,000. You sold the note (or surrendered it as collateral) for $70,000. The GPR (gross profit ratio) on the property sale was 0.6384 (needed for determining the "income attributable"). What is your tax basis in the note?

The basis is—

Unpaid portion of note	$85,000
LESS	
Income attributable to unpaid portion	
• $85,000 x 0.6384	<54,264>
Basis =	$30,736

If the note were sold for $70,000, the gain would be:

$70,000 – 30,736 (basis)　　　　=　　$39,264 Gain

If, for some reason, the note became unenforceable and uncollectible after being paid down to $85,000, its fair market value would be zero. Hence, the loss would be:

$0 – 30,736 (basis)　　　　　　=　　$30,736 Loss

When modifying, substituting, or altering the terms of an installment obligation, extreme care should be exercised to avoid the change being characterized as a disposition. Any increase or decrease in face value is treated as a disposition. But changing payment dates or rates of interest (without changing face value) is not a disposition.

A "disposition" triggers the completion of Form 6252 as though the installment note were satisfied in full. Then, *separately*, the gain or loss on disposition of the note would be reported on Schedule D or Form 4797, whichever is applicable. The character of the gain or loss would depend on the tax character of the property sale from which the note derived.

12

OTHER DISPOSITIONS

After An Active Life Of Rental Property
Exchanges And Tax Postponements, There
Comes A Time To "Bite The Bullet." Leaving All
Decisions To Your Heirs Will Guarantee
Maximum Tax. Once You Realize This, You
Begin To Appreciate The Feature Role Of Form
4797: SALES OF BUSINESS PROPERTY.
Using This Form Gives You The Benefits Of
Section 1231: Capital Gain/Ordinary Loss.
There Are At Least 8 Different Strategies For
Softening And Diluting The Final Tax Bite.
Depositing Your After-Tax Cash Proceeds Into
TAX-FREE MUNICIPAL FUNDS Is A Glorious
Way To Enjoy Life In Retirement.

For some property owners, real estate gets into their blood.
There, it becomes a life-long addiction as a means for amassing
power and wealth, or at least for building a comfortable nest egg for
retirement and old age. Rental real estate is especially addictive in
this regard because it—

1. Generates income while being held.
2. Has significant tax benefits.
3. Generally appreciates in value.

For life-long investment goals, rental real estate offers benefits
which are unmatched by any other single class of investment. While
the tax rules on operating loss limitations have imposed some
restrictions on overzealous property owners, the loss carryover

accounting required actually becomes a strategic advantage for owners of multiple properties. The loss limitation rules benefit those who intentionally dispose of their property periodically.

Our contention has been all along that the ideal multi-property ownership is three to five properties at any one time. Furthermore, for best tax opportunities, each property should be disposed of every three to five years. The tax rules change so much that this is the only way to keep ahead of the game. In a property investment lifespan of some 30 to 50 years, this means approximately 10 dispositions of property in one's active tax lifetime.

In this chapter, therefore, we want to focus on the disposition taxing of rental property, and to acquaint you with the tax effects of depreciation recapture. We want to thoroughly familiarize you with **Form 4797**: Sales of Business Property, and to stress its importance as a focal summary of all property disposition for each taxable year. Whereas Schedule E is your principal form to use while holding and renting your properties, Form 4797 is the form to use when disposing of *any* of your properties.

Death Tax Consequences

A common stance among those who have real estate in their blood is that it is up to their children and heirs to worry about the tax consequences when the property owner dies. Except for small estates, almost invariably those who inherit the property have to sell at least some of it, to pay the death tax thereon. By a "small estate," we mean where the aggregate FMV of all properties, including the decedent's personal residence, does not exceed $600,000. Holding three to five rental properties, plus one's personal residence (and possibly also a vacation home) can easily exceed this amount.

Once your gross estate is over $600,000, the Federal death tax bite mounts astonishingly. It **starts at 37%** for estates over $600,000. It reaches up to 55% for estates over $3,000,000.

For multi-property owners, gross estates over $1,000,000 are quite common these days. During life, you may not live and feel like you are worth over a million dollars. But, upon death, the final tax blow comes down hard. Do not overlook this fact in your eagerness to avoid, during life, ever disposing of your rental properties.

The IRS's death tax return is **Form 706**: U.S. Estate Tax Return. It is a 35-page tax form! The very first schedule attached to this form is Schedule A: **Real Estate**. A headnote to this schedule refers you to sections 2032 and 2032A of the tax code.

Section 2032 allows the executor of your estate to elect to value the property at six months after your death. Otherwise, the date of valuation is fixed at date of death. Section 2032A allows your executor to discount the valuation up to $750,000 if more than 50% of your real estate was used in any rental or farming business. Death taxes apply to the FMV of property: NOT to one's cost or other basis in that property.

Your death tax MUST BE PAID. Except for limited extensions of time to pay, no after-death strategies apply for diluting said tax.

Related Party Dispositions

If you dispose of property by sale or exchange to a family member or to a related entity, the transaction becomes suspect. The suspicion is that the transaction will take place at a price below its true fair market value. The suspicion assumes that the seller is in a high tax bracket and is motivated strictly by tax reasons. The suspicion also assumes that there has been some prearrangement with the related person or entity (who is in a lower tax bracket) to resell the property to a third party at its fair market value.

Because of these suspicions, there are three particular tax code sections that you should be aware of. These are:

Sec. 267(a) — Loss Transactions Between Related Taxpayers
- No deduction is allowed for any loss with respect to the sale or exchange of property.

Sec. 453(e) — Second Dispositions by Related Persons
- If gain property is sold to a related person, and that person disposes of it within 2 years, all gain is taxable to the first transferor.

Sec. 1031(f) — Exchanges Between Related Persons
- If property is exchanged, and the related person disposes of such property within 2 years, there is no deferment of gain to the first person.

On Forms 6252 (installment sales) and 8824 (exchanges), you are pointedly asked:

- Was the property sold to (or exchanged with) a related party? ☐ Yes ☐ No

- If "Yes," did the related party sell, resell, or dispose of the property within 2 years of the first disposition? ☐ Yes ☐ No

- If "Yes," pay all tax on the sale or exchange. ☐

Our recommendation, of course, is to refrain from dispositions to related persons, unless the transaction is truly at arm's length in a fair market. Even then, a two-year restriction on resale should be one of the contractual terms of the first disposition.

Section 1231 Dispositions

As a long-term rental property owner, there is another section of the tax code that you should be aware of. This is Section **1231**. (Do not confuse with Section **1031**.) Section 1231 carries the official heading: ***Property Used in the Trade or Business and Involuntary Conversions***. For property held more than one year, Section 1231 is known as the "capital gain, ordinary loss" rule. It is the *ordinary loss* feature of this rule that is particularly useful to us.

Subsection 1231(a)(3)(B) defines a "Section 1231 loss" as—

Any recognized loss from a sale or exchange . . . of property . . . held for more than 1 year . . . in connection with a trade or business . . . or from the compulsory or involuntary conversion [of such property].

Subsection 1231(a)(4)(A) then goes on to say—

The section 1231 losses shall be included only if and to the extent taken into account in computing taxable income, except that section 1211 shall not apply.

What are these statutory words saying?

They are saying that if you incur a bona fide loss from the sale, exchange, or involuntary conversion of rental real estate, there is no limitation to the deductibility of this loss, other than to the extent of your taxable income. You can drive your taxable income to zero, but not negative. In other words, Section 1231 losses can be used to offset all other forms of tax accountable income, **without** the limitations we told you about in Chapter 5.

"But," you ask, "What's the Section 1211 bit all about?"

Section 1211(b) limits *capital* losses for individuals to $3,000 per year. By decreeing for Section 1231 purposes that Section 1211 does not apply, the tax code has recharacterized rental property from a capital asset to ordinary loss property in disposition loss situations. This recharacterization bypasses all of the passive activity loss rules ordinarily associated with rental property. This recharacterization is a powerful tax advantage if, indeed, you have bona fide losses at time of disposition of the property.

Importance of Form 4797

Whereas Schedule E (Part I) is the single most important tax form when holding and renting real estate, Form 4797: **Sales of Business Property** is the single most important tax form when *disposing* of any of your rental properties. We barely touched on Form 4797 in Chapters 10 (Section 1031 Exchanges) and 11 (Installment Sales). Now, we want to stress its importance when disposing of business property in any manner. Once a property is listed on Schedule E, the only way it can get off of that schedule is via Form 4797.

Form 4797 is a collective/summary form for all disposition transactions involving property held for productive business purposes. It is not limited to rental real estate. It accommodates direct sales, installment sales, like-kind exchanges, involuntary conversions, casualty losses, Section 1231 losses, recapture income, depreciation recapture, and other (ordinary) gains and losses. In addition to direct entries on the form itself, it includes information from other supporting forms, and combines, nets, and recharacterizes certain gains and losses. It then directs the transfer of capital gain information to Schedule D (1040) and the transfer of ordinary gain/loss information to page 1 of Form 1040.

To help you visualize the central dispositional role of Form 4797, we present Figure 12.1. Note that we identify a new form that we have never before mentioned. It is Form 4684: *Casualties*

Supplemental Forms

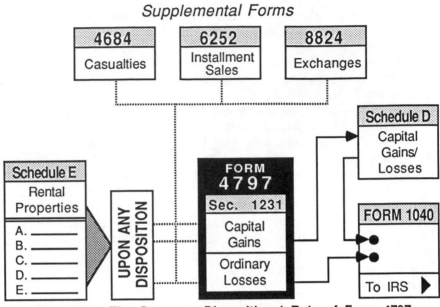

Fig. 12.1 - The Summary Dispositional Role of Form 4797

and Thefts. With respect to rental real estate, casualties are those occurring from fire, storm, and other natural disasters. Thefts are the financial consequences of fraud, misrepresentation, and unconscionable lawsuits.

The applicable tax law on casualties and thefts is Section 165: *Losses*. The general rule thereunder is subsection 165(a), to wit:

> *There shall be allowed as a deduction any loss sustained during the taxable year and not compensated for by insurance or otherwise.*

Subsection 165(b) addresses the gain or loss from the subsection (a) compensation as though the property were disposed of at its adjusted tax basis.

Section B of Form 4684 addresses business and income-producing property only. It accommodates up to four properties at one time. The compensation gains and losses are netted, and then partitioned into capital gain and ordinary gain/loss amounts. The capital gain amounts go onto Part I of Form 4797; the ordinary gain/loss amounts go onto Part II of Form 4797.

Form 4797 is also useful for post-dispositional transactions. Even after a parcel of property is disposed of, litigation can arise, involuntary reacquisition can occur, and unforeseen matters can emerge. There is sufficient space in parts I and II of Form 4797 to enter virtually any type of transactional computation affecting rental real estate. For disposition tax accounting, Form 4797 is THE FORM to use.

Form 4797: Parts I and II

There are actually three parts to Form 4797. Parts I and II take up one page; Part III takes up a separate page of its own. The edited and abbreviated headings of these parts are:

I — Sales, Exchanges, or Conversions: More Than 1 Year
II — Ordinary Gains and Losses
III — Gain from Disposition of Recapture Property

Entries in Parts I and II differ primarily by the holding period of the property involved. Part I is only for dispositions of property held more than one year. Otherwise, Part II is used. Part II is also used for any other dispositional transaction that doesn't fit elsewhere on your return. Part II is a good catchall.

The reason for the distinction between Parts I and II is the Section 1231 disposition rule. If a net gain results from aggregating the gains and losses from those properties held more than one year, the result is treated as as *capital* gain. If the aggregate result is a net loss, the amount is treated as an *ordinary* loss. If there is a net loss in Part I, it is automatically directed into Part II.

With the above generalities as background, we present in Figure 12.2 a stripped-down version of parts I and II of Form 4797.

Formatwise, each part is similar. The upper portion accommodates direct entries; the lower portion accommodates indirect entries. Direct entries are those for which the computational essentials are shown directly on the face of Form 4797 itself. These computations appear nowhere else on your return. Indirect entries are the summary amounts — gain or loss — from computational entries on other forms which attach to your tax return. We urge you to read through the indirect entry lines carefully. They tell you in a few words much of what goes on in the property disposition world.

In each of Parts I and II, there is a "netting" line (emphasized in Figure 12.2). This line is preceded by a line which displays, in two

Form 4797	SALES OF BUSINESS PROPERTY					Tax	Year
Individuals : Attach To Form 1040							
PART I - Property Held More Than 1 Year							
(a)	(b)	(c)	(d)	(e)	(f)	(g)	(h)
				DEPR.		LOSS	GAIN
DIRECT ENTRIES							
● Gain from Form 4684						▨	
● Gain from Form 6252						▨	
● Gain from Form 8824						▨	
● Capital Gain, Part III						▨	
● Sec.1231 losses: prior years							▨
ADD COLUMNS (g) AND (h): NET ▶							
IF GAIN, enter on Schedule D IF LOSS, enter on Part II							
PART II - Ordinary Gains and Losses							
DIRECT ENTRIES							
● Loss from Part I							▨
● Recapture Sec. 1231 gain						▨	
● Recapture Income, Part III						▨	
● Gain/Loss from Form 4684							
● Ordinary Gain, Form 6252						▨	
ADD COLUMNS (g) AND (h): NET ▶							
Enter on Form 1040, Page 1							

Fig. 12.2 - General Arrangement of Form 4797: Parts I and II

separate columns, the subtotal gains and subtotal losses. Every disposition event for the year is pulled together, summarized, and netted at this point. Other than for installment sales, once a dispositional entry for a particular property appears on Form 4797, it thereafter "disappears" from your subsequent-year tax returns.

Form 4797: Part III

In Figure 12.2, there is a line in Part I designated as *Capital gain, Part III* and in Part II a line designated as *Recapture income, Part III*. Before entries in either of these lines can be computed, Part III of Form 4797 needs to be explained. Part III appears on the reverse side (page 2) of the official form.

Officially, Part III is titled: **Gain From Dispositions of Property Under Sections 1245, 1250, 1252, 1254, and 1255.** All of these tax code sections identify what we classify as "recapture property." While said properties were being held, certain special writeoffs were allowed for depreciation, conservation expenditures, and government subsidies. When the benefited property is disposed of, the previous writeoffs are recaptured as ordinary income. The use of Part III for computing the amount of recapture is for *gain* dispositions only, and only if the property has been held more than one year.

A thumbnail sketch of each of the five recapture property classes follows:

Sec. 1245 — Depreciable tangible property (such as furniture, appliances, machinery, equipment, etc.) for which *any* kind of depreciation was taken.

Sec. 1250 — Depreciable real property (such as buildings, structures, and their improvements) for which *additional* (meaning "accelerated") depreciation was taken.

Sec. 1252 — Farmland held for less than 10 years for which conservation expenditures (such as soil, water, and reforestation efforts) were expensed rather than capitalized.

Sec. 1254 — Resource land on which intangible drilling and development costs were expensed rather than amortized over 10 years or more.

Sec. 1255 — Farmland held for less than 20 years for which government subsidy payments were previously excluded from gross income.

For instructional purposes, we present in Figure 12.3 a highly simplified version of Part III: Form 4797. We just want to familiarize you with its general format. It accommodates four separate properties. The total gain on each property is computed

Form 4797	GAIN FROM DISPOSITION OF RECAPTURE PROPERTY	Part III
	Under Sections 1245, 1250, 1252, 1254, 1255	

Description of Property • Each separate property element	"A"	"B"
• Held more than 1 year • Date acquired; date sold	"C"	"D"

Computation of Gain
   1. Gross sales price
   2. Cost or other basis plus expense of sale
   3. Depreciation allowed or allowable
   4. Adjusted basis: subtract 3 from 2
   5. Total gain: subtract 4 from 1	

• **Section 1245**
   - Depreciation of machinery & equipment
• **Section 1250**
   - Additional depreciation of buildings
• **Section 1252**
   - Conservation expenses: farmland
• **Section 1254**
   - Intangible drilling & development costs
• **Section 1255**
   - Subsidy payments excluded from income	

Summary of part III Gains
   6. Total gain all properties ....
   7. Total of recapture income
      • Enter here & on Part II (ordinary) ....
   8. Subtract 7 from 6
      • Enter here & on Part I (capital) ....
	_____
	
	_____
	
	_____

Fig. 12.3 - General Arrangement of Form 4797: Part III

separately in a simplified 5-step sequence of its own. We show these five steps in the upper half of Figure 12.3.

At the bottom of Figure 12.3, there are three steps showing how the total gain from all properties is split between recapture income (ordinary gain) and capital gain. As indicated, the capital gain goes onto Part I and the recapture income goes onto Part II.

Illustrative Recapture Example

Let us illustrate the concept of depreciation recapture as it applies to separate classes (elements) of improvements to real property. To do so, consider that a 5-plex (five dwelling units) residential rental complex was purchased some years ago for $180,000. Its purchase contract allocated the $180,000 as follows:

	$	%
Land	35,000	19.44
Building(s)	110,000	61.12
Pool, etc.	25,000	13.88
Appliances	10,000	5.56
	180,000	100.00%

Assume that the property was recently sold for $350,000; the selling expenses were $35,000. At the time of the sale, the basis in the building was $50,000. The $60,000 depreciation writeoff (110,000 cost - 50,000 basis) consisted of $35,000 straight-line depreciation and $25,000 of additional (accelerated) depreciation. The pool and its equipment had a basis of $10,000; the dwelling unit appliances had a basis of $2,500. What are the allocable recapture aspects here?

First, we have to allocate the gross sale price to each of the four separate elements of the realty. Thus,

Land	=	19.44% x $350,000	=	$ 68,040
Building(s)	=	61.12% x 350,000	=	213,920
Pool, etc.	=	13.88% x 350,000	=	48,580
Appliances	=	5.56% x 350,000	=	19,460
				$350,000

Next, we need to do the same allocation for the selling expenses. Since we deliberately chose the selling expenses to be 10% of the selling price, the allocations would be: land 6,804; building 21,392; pool 4,858; and appliances 1,946.

Next, we must compute the gain separately on each of the four elements of the property parcel. Using the 5-step sequence in Figure 12.3, each gain is as follows:

Land	=	$ 26,236
Building(s)	=	142,528

Pool, etc.   =   33,722
Appliances =   <u>15,014</u>
              $217,500   Total gain

Even though the land itself does not depreciate (and, therefore, there is no recapture income from it), we must establish its gain, so that there will be a proper allocation of the total gain among all elements of the sale.

The dwelling unit appliances, and the pool and its equipment, constitute "Section 1245 property." Therefore, all of their depreciation — whether accelerated or straight line — is recaptured as ordinary income. For the illustration given, the respective recapture income amounts are:

- Pool, etc.   [25,000 cost – 10,000 basis] = $15,000 *depr*
- Appliances [10,000 cost – 2,500 basis] =   <u>7,500</u> *depr*
                          Sec. 1245 = $22,500

The 5-plex building and its improvements constitute "Section 1250 property." This splits the total depreciation between its straight-line portion and its additional (accelerated) portion. For the illustration given, these portions are $35,000 and $25,000, respectively: total $60,000. It is only the additional depreciation (above straight-line) that is recaptured as ordinary income. Therefore, the Section 1250 portion is $25,000.

Hence, the entries in the lower portion of Figure 12.3 would be as follows:

Total gain all properties	$217,500	
Total of recapture income		
• Sec. 1245	<22,500>	
• Sec. 1250	<u><25,000></u>	▶ Part II
Net capital gain	$170,000	▶ Part I

As an aside note, even though the $35,000 of straight-line depreciation on the building(s) does not show up as recapture income, it, nevertheless, does show up as recapture gain. Because of the 5-step computational sequence required, the total depreciation taken reduces the adjusted basis when the property is sold. This automatically increases the total gain. The net result is that *all depreciation* at time of sale is recaptured either as ordinary income, capital gain, or a combination of both.

"Bite the Bullet" Time

After 30 years or so of acquiring, renting, depreciating, and exchanging rental properties, you now have five properties totaling 12 dwelling units, as depicted in Figure 12.4. Since your children are not interested in owning any of your five rentals, you decide that it might be time to bite the bullet and pay the tax on all of your deferred gains . . . plus any current capital gains. You still don't want to pay any more tax than you absolutely have to. What is a good approach to your "phasing out" decision? Are there any objective strategies to be employed?

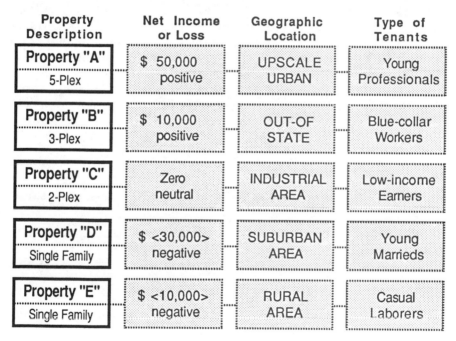

Property Description	Net Income or Loss	Geographic Location	Type of Tenants
Property "A" 5-Plex	$ 50,000 positive	UPSCALE URBAN	Young Professionals
Property "B" 3-Plex	$ 10,000 positive	OUT-OF STATE	Blue-collar Workers
Property "C" 2-Plex	Zero neutral	INDUSTRIAL AREA	Low-income Earners
Property "D" Single Family	$ <30,000> negative	SUBURBAN AREA	Young Marrieds
Property "E" Single Family	$ <10,000> negative	RURAL AREA	Casual Laborers

Fig. 12.4 - Assumed Property Holdings for Phase-Out Strategies

Yes, there are at least eight strategies that you can employ.

First, you pick one of the properties (in Figure 12.4) that is to be the last to be disposed of. Pick the one that is the best income producer, causes you the least tenant problems, and has good appreciation potential. This would be Property A — the 5-plex. A multi-dwelling-unit property in an urban area, accessible to young professionals, tends to be choice investment property. Such property is easy to sell or exchange. If there are no rent controls in the area, keep such property to the bitter end. This is "Strategy 1."

Your second strategy is to organize and review your tax records and tax basis in all properties that you hold. Plan to dispose of them all — one at a time. Mull things over, and decide to go for the first cash opportunity that comes along. This is "Strategy 2."

First Disposition: All Cash

Out of the blue, one day, you receive a letter by certified mail from the XYZ Airport Authority where your Property C (in Figure 12.4) is located. You are officially told that your property will be condemned for an airport expansion project. You are informed that you can either negotiate a price now or wait until the condemnation process is complete, at which time you have to accept the judicially decreed price: called "condemnation award."

You talk things over with your tax advisor. He tells you about Section 1033: Involuntary Conversions, and about paragraphs (1) *Conversion into similar property* and (2) *Conversion into money*. He also tells you that you have up to three years after receiving the condemnation award to replace the converted property with similar or like-kind property. [Sec. 1033(g)(1), (4).]

Fate, it seems is testing your will. Do you take the condemnation award, pocket it, and pay the tax, or do you "roll it over" into comparable rental property elsewhere?

Once a public project and its eminent domain proceedings become general knowledge in an area, property values tumble. Government agencies and their legal agents know this. They use this phenomenon to take advantage of you, whether you try to negotiate a price or wait until the condemnation proceedings are final. Our suggestion is that you get your money (on your own or with an attorney) before the rest of the affected property owners get theirs. Whether by negotiation or judicial award, condemnation proceeds are paid in cash. At the time of payment, you must surrender title to the property to the condemning authority.

This brings us to "Strategy 3." Decide in advance where you are going to deposit — and retain — the gross proceeds from your first cash sale. You want to build up a nest egg that is not going to be depleted with further taxes. For this reason, we suggest a tax-free — *truly* tax free — account with an established mutual fund. Consult your mutual fund advisor on this matter.

"Strategy 4": Problem Properties

With an all-cash disposition experience under your belt — and your taxes, which you've postponed all of these years, paid — a new feeling emerges. You now have some money in reserve earning tax-free income. You are no longer "property rich and cash poor" as you've been in the past. You now have time to select and prioritize the problem properties that you want to get rid of. This is your "Strategy 4."

In Figure 12.4, there are three target properties for consideration. Property A is to be held to the end. Property C has been cashed out. This leaves properties B, D, and E for disposition consideration.

Property B is a triplex (three separate dwelling units) located out of your state of domicile. It earns some net positive income. This means that you've had to file a nonresident state income tax return all of the years that you've been holding it. It's in a "gross-up" nonresident state like California. You're getting tired of being hassled by the out-of-state taxing agency. Besides, the property needs some major improvements and renovations. The property management fees keep increasing every year, out of step with your modest rent increases. Property B becomes your first priority for disposition.

Property D is a single family rental in a nice suburban area. The tenants are young parents who want to own their own home someday. You bought the property only a few years ago, and paid top dollar for it. You have it mortgaged to the hilt (to 80% of its market value). It serves a metropolitan area where the capital appreciation has been modest but steady. It's in a price range (under $300,000) that will sell when you are ready. Its only problem is that it is a money loser. This is acceptable as long as you hold Property A. The loss from D can be used to offset the profit from A. Thus, it becomes your next-to-last property to dispose of.

Property E is also a single family rental, but it is in a rural area where the economy is intermittent and slow. You bought it very cheaply; the rents are low; and you've depreciated it down to near zero. Your tenants are casual laborers. Though honest and hardworking, they have a difficult time making ends meet. The rent is often late or skipped altogether. Out of the goodness of your heart, you have forgiven the rent from time to time. When the tenants are out of work, you supply paint and material, and they supply the labor to spruce up the property. Property E becomes your second priority for disposition, after Property B.

Out-of-State Exchanges

"Strategy 5" is to exchange your out-of-state property (B above) for in-state property. To do this successfully, you prepare for a *down exchange*. That is, the like-kind replacement property in-state is less in value than the relinquished property out-of-state. There are reasons for this.

Property B is desirable exchange property because it produces positive cash flow. Because it is a rental triplex, it will be difficult to sell outright. Too much cash and extensive renovations are needed. You figure the property is worth $350,000 at least. If you get any out-of-state buy offer at all, it'll be for minimal down (like $10,000) with you taking a wrap-around note for $340,000. So, you're going to have to make some concessions to get the property off of your hands. This is why the down exchange.

In a down exchange, you'll have to pay some tax — NOT on the full realized gain — to the nonresident state. This is desirable because you want to file a "final return" with that state. When the exchange is complete, your in-state property replacement will not be under the legal jurisdiction of the nonresident state.

Since 1986, when there was a major overhaul of the federal tax laws, many states now class themselves as *conforming states*. This means that they accept the federal law (Section 1031) on tax deferred exchanges as satisfying their own state tax laws. This is because you attach your federal return to the nonresident state return. So, when you make a down-exchange, you pay the nonresident state tax (as well as federal) on the recognized gain, and automatically disclose to the nonresident state your in-state replacement property. Thereafter, there is no provision for the nonresident state to keep tracking your in-state property acquired in the exchange. Whether this is a loophole or not is another matter.

Your in-state replacement rental should be a single family residence. Single family residences are easier to sell. The occupant owners can get maximum mortgage coverage and often can arrange with their employer credit unions for second mortgages.

Once the down-exchange is complete, there is no reason why you should not immediately put the in-state replacement up for sale. After all, the exchange is not a related party transaction. You are not bound by any two-year restriction on the resale. Get the best top dollar that you can. Pay the tax, and shove more money into your tax-free nest egg.

Charitable or Public Gifting

As to Property E above — the rural area single family rental — you have to employ an entirely different strategy. It is undesirable exchange property (no positive cash flow) and it is unlikely to be saleable unless you take back 100% of the financing. You don't want to do this. Then, suddenly, a bright idea strikes you. Why not donate the property to a charitable cause?

Why not? Why not "Strategy 6"?

There *are* tax advantages in donating appreciated capital gain property to charity (remember your tax basis is near zero). Tax Code Section 170: *Charitable, Etc., Contributions and Gifts*, allows you to take a personal (nonbusiness) deduction on Schedule A (Form 1040) for the *full FMV* of the donated real estate. You get the deduction and you don't pay tax on the capital gain, either! There are tricky rules and limits involved, especially Section 170(e) and its regulations. So, check this out with your own tax advisor. The principal catch is that the donated property must be used regularly for the charitable organization's exempt function.

Once you decide on which charitable organization to give to, get hold of IRS **Form 8283: Noncash Charitable Contributions**. Turn to Section B thereof: Appraisal Summary. This section of Form 8283 is for donated property of more than $5,000 FMV. Property E, you estimate, is worth at least $65,000 and maybe as high as $80,000. Locate a real estate appraiser serving the area, pay his fee, and have him professionally value the property. Then have him sign Part III of Section B: Certification of Appraiser. Subsequently, have the charitable organization sign Part IV of Section B: Donee Acknowledgment.

Usually, the donee organization will provide legal assistance for preparing a Gift Deed for transferring title of your property to the charitable organization. Once the gift deed is recorded, and you have Form 8283 completed, you have a bona fide charitable contribution deduction on your personal Schedule A (Itemized Deductions). An entry amount of $65,000 to $80,000 is substantial enough to offset (at least partially) the capital gain on other property that you might sell during the gift year.

"Strategy 7": Next-to-Last

We have already set you up for what we call your "next-to-last" rental property disposition. This is Property D above: the money loser. It is also fully mortgaged. However, the property is in a good and growing area of single-family home owners. There are good schools nearby. Your tenants are a young married couple with two preschool-age children. They tell you that they are beginning to look around to buy their own home. At this point, "Strategy 7" comes on line.

You approach the young couple who have been paying their rent regularly and say:

"Look, if you can qualify for the existing mortgage payments, and drum up some additional cash on your own, I'll offer to sell the place to you at the low end of a professionally appraised market price. If you are interested, and we work together on this, we don't need a real estate agent or an attorney. This will save us both money. We can go to the title (escrow) company together and give them our instructions. If you can't come up with all of the necessary cash down (to the existing mortgage), I'll take back a second mortgage for three to five years."

Or words to this effect.

The idea here is that you offer your good paying tenants first opportunity to buy your next-to-last rental property. You can make the terms reasonable, yet on the low side, because they are not members of your own family. Often this approach does work. If it works, you consummate the sale. If not, offer similar terms to the open market through a real estate broker. Again, put your after-tax money from the sale into your tax-free nest egg account.

Your "Final" Exchange

You are now left with Property A in Figure 12.4. This is that good money maker, the 5-plex, which is accessible to an upscale metropolitan area. Its excellent positive cash flow makes it a highly desirable property for exchanging. Being a multi-unit rental complex, it is unlikely that you could sell it for all cash, even if you tried. So, judicious exchanging is your only practical option.

By "judicious exchanging" we mean converting the 5-plex into *multiple*, *separate*, *single-family* residences. For example, target the conversion into three to five single-family residences in prime suburban locations. Multiple separate properties give you greater tax planning flexibility than having all of your gold in one large property pot. This is "Strategy 8": the fan-out, phase-out of your property holdings, as illustrated in Figure 12.5.

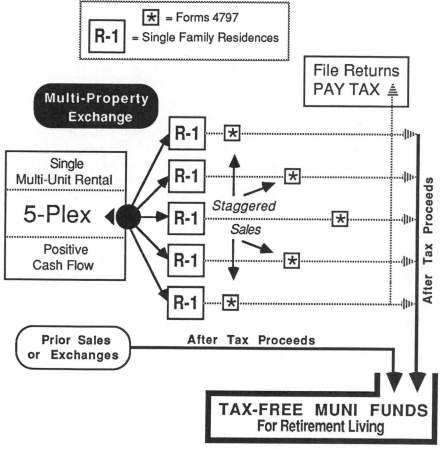

Fig. 12.5 - Final "Fan-Out" of Property Dispositions

The fan-out, phase-out strategy is to avert an 8.0 or higher Richter scale tax shock on your final property disposition(s). You acquire from three to five replacement properties with the full intention of selling them, one at a time. By doing so, you diffuse the tax bang all along the way. Whether you exchange up or down is irrelevant. This is your last exchange.

At this stage in your life, you want top dollar for each of the replacement property sales. If you have to take an installment note on one or more of the offered properties, limit the duration of the note to five years at most. Insert a "balloon payment" clause (full balance due) at that time. You just don't want the default risks that accompany 10-, 20-, or 30-year installment notes.

Because of the transfer-of-basis rules (back in Figure 10.4), exchanged properties enjoy what is called the "tack on" of holding periods [Sec. 1223(1)]. This means that if you can tax trace the exchanged properties back, say, 10 years (or whatever), the holding period of the most recently acquired replacement property (such as in Figure 12.5) is 10 years (or whatever). By *inflation indexing* your tax basis over this number of years, you can significantly enhance your "adjusted" return of capital. One of the hidden benefits of capital gain taxing is that your return of capital is NOT TAXED. This is why *cost or other basis, plus improvements and expenses of sale* are so important when you prepare Form 4797 for each fanned-out property. Be sure to take advantage of the reduced capital gain tax rates for sales occurring after August 5, 1997 (*Taxpayer Relief Act*).

As the cash from each final sale comes in, and after paying all of the capital gains tax thereon, stuff more and more of your money into your tax-free nest egg account. By the time your final-final sale is complete, you will have built up an impressive nest egg — **well over** $1,000,000 (1 million). What a glorious feeling it is to live in retirement on truly tax-free income.

"Happy selling" to you!

ABOUT
THE AUTHOR

Holmes F. Crouch

Born on a small farm in southern Maryland, Holmes was graduated from the U.S. Coast Guard Academy with a Bachelor's Degree in Marine Engineering. While serving on active duty, he wrote many technical articles on maritime matters. After attaining the rank of Lieutenant Commander, he resigned to pursue a career as a nuclear engineer.

Continuing his education, he earned a Master's Degree in Nuclear Engineering from the University of California. He also authored two books on nuclear propulsion. As a result of the tax write-offs associated with writing these books, the IRS audited his returns. The IRS's handling of the audit procedure so annoyed Holmes that he undertook to become as knowledgeable as possible regarding tax procedures. He became a licensed private Tax Practitioner by passing an examination administered by the IRS. Having attained this credential, he started his own tax preparation and counseling business in 1972.

In the early years of his tax practice, he was a regular talk-show guest on San Francisco's KGO Radio responding to hundreds of phone-in tax questions from listeners. He was a much sought-after guest speaker at many business seminars and taxpayer meetings. He also provided counseling on special tax problems, such as divorce matters, property exchanges, timber harvesting, mining ventures, animal breeding, independent contractors, selling businesses, and offices-at-home. Over the past 25 years, he has prepared nearly 10,000 tax returns for individuals, estates, trusts, and small businesses (in partnership and corporate form).

During the tax season of January through April, he prepares returns in a unique manner. During a single meeting, he completes the return . . . *on the spot!* The client leaves with his return signed, sealed, and in a stamped envelope. His unique approach to preparing returns and his personal interest in his clients' tax affairs have honed his professional proficiency. His expertise extends through itemized deductions, computer-matching of income sources, capital gains and losses, business expenses and cost of goods, residential rental expenses, limited and general partnership activities, closely-held corporations, to family farms and ranches.

He remembers spending 12 straight hours completing a doctor's complex return. The next year, the doctor, having moved away, utilized a large accounting firm to prepare his return. Their accountant was so impressed by the manner in which the prior return was prepared that he recommended the doctor travel the 500 miles each year to have Holmes continue doing it.

He recalls preparing a return for an unemployed welder, for which he charged no fee. Two years later the welder came back and had his return prepared. He paid the regular fee . . . and then added a $300 tip.

During the off season, he represents clients at IRS audits and appeals. In one case a shoe salesman's audit was scheduled to last three hours. However, after examining Holmes' documentation it was concluded in 15 minutes with "no change" to his return. In another instance he went to an audit of a custom jeweler that the IRS dragged out for more than six hours. But, supported by Holmes' documentation, the client's return was accepted by the IRS with "no change."

Then there was the audit of a language translator that lasted two full days. The auditor scrutinized more than $1.25 million in gross receipts, all direct costs, and operating expenses. Even though all expensed items were documented and verified, the auditor decided that more than $23,000 of expenses ought to be listed as capital items for depreciation instead. If this had been enforced it would have resulted in a significant additional amount of tax. Holmes strongly disagreed and after many hours explanation got the amount reduced by more than 60% on behalf of his client.

He has dealt extensively with gift, death and trust tax returns. These preparations have involved him in the tax aspects of wills, estate planning, trustee duties, probate, marital and charitable bequests, gift and death exemptions, and property titling.

Although not an attorney, he prepares Petitions to the U.S. Tax Court for clients. He details the IRS errors and taxpayer facts by citing pertinent sections of tax law and regulations. In a recent case involving an attorney's ex-spouse, the IRS asserted a tax deficiency of $155,000. On behalf of his client, he petitioned the Tax Court and within six months the IRS conceded the case.

Over the years, Holmes has observed that the IRS is not the industrious, impartial, and competent federal agency that its official public imaging would have us believe.

He found that, at times, under the slightest pretext, the IRS has interpreted against a taxpayer in order to assess maximum penalties, and may even delay pending matters so as to increase interest due on additional taxes. He has confronted the IRS in his own behalf on five separate occasions, going before the U.S. Claims Court, U.S. District Court, and U.S. Tax Court. These were court actions that tested specific sections of the Internal Revenue Code which he found ambiguous, inequitable, and abusively interpreted by the IRS.

Disturbed by the conduct of the IRS and by the general lack of tax knowledge by most individuals, he began an innovative series of taxpayer-oriented Federal tax guides. To fulfill this need, he undertook the writing of a series of guidebooks that provide in-depth knowledge on one tax subject at a time. He focuses on subjects that plague taxpayers all throughout the year. Hence, his formulation of the "Allyear" Tax Guide series.

The author is indebted to his wife, Irma Jean, and daughter, Barbara MacRae, for the word processing and computer graphics that turn his experiences into the reality of these publications. Holmes welcomes comments, questions, and suggestions from his readers. He can be contacted in California at (408) 867-2628, or by writing to the publisher's address.

ALLYEAR Tax Guides
by Holmes F. Crouch

For information about the above titles,
and/or a free 8 page catalog, contact:

www.allyeartax.com

Phone: (408) 867-2628   Fax: (408) 867-6466